TOM BLOOM

ELLYN SPRAGINS
is an award-winning
journalist whose work
has appeared in *News-
week, Bloomberg Per-
sonal, Business Week,*
and *Forbes.* A leading
reporter and writer
on health care, she pioneered consumer
rankings of HMOs for *Bloomberg Personal*
and for *Newsweek*'s June 1996 cover story,
"America's Best HMOs," the first to
appear in national magazines.

"This book **GIVES CONSUMERS THE INFORMATION AND UNDERSTANDING THEY NEED TO MAKE INFORMED DECISIONS** about their health care."

STANLEY BREZENOFF
President and CEO
Maimonides Medical Center

"**A WEALTH OF USEFUL INFORMATION. THOUGHTFUL AND RIGHT ON TARGET.**"

BRUCE BRADLEY
Director, Managed Care Plans
General Motors

"**A MUST-READ** for employers, employees, and, indeed, all consumers of health care. . . An **UNBIASED AND EASY-TO-READ GUIDE . . .**"

TIMOTHY N. TROY
Editor in Chief
Managed Healthcare

"Spragins has done a good job of translating the often complex language of managed care into text consumers can understand. *Choosing and Using an HMO* is a **USEFUL RESOURCE FOR ANYONE INTERESTED IN HEALTH CARE QUALITY.**"

MARGARET E. O'KANE
President
National Committee for Quality Assurance

Choosing and Using an HMO

Also available from
THE BLOOMBERG PERSONAL BOOKSHELF

Smarter Insurance Solutions
by Janet Bamford

Smart Questions to Ask Your Financial Advisers
by Lynn Brenner

Investing in Small-Cap Stocks
by Christopher Graja and
Elizabeth Ungar, Ph.D.

A Commonsense Guide to Mutual Funds
by Mary Rowland

A Commonsense Guide to Your 401(k)
by Mary Rowland
(December 1997)

BLOOMBERG PERSONAL BOOKSHELF

Choosing and Using an HMO

ELLYN SPRAGINS

ILLUSTRATIONS BY ADAM McCAULEY

BLOOMBERG PRESS
PRINCETON

Books are available for bulk purchases at special discounts. Special editions or book excerpts can also be created to specifications. For information, please write: Special Markets Department, Bloomberg Press.

BLOOMBERG, THE BLOOMBERG, BLOOMBERG BUSINESS NEWS, BLOOMBERG NEWS, BLOOMBERG FINANCIAL MARKETS, BLOOMBERG PRESS, BLOOMBERG PROFESSIONAL LIBRARY, and BLOOMBERG PERSONAL BOOKSHELF are trademarks and service marks of Bloomberg L.P. All rights reserved.

This publication contains the author's opinions and is designed to provide accurate and authoritative information. It is sold with the understanding that the author, publisher, and Bloomberg L.P. are not engaged in rendering legal, health care, accounting, investment-planning, or other professional advice. The reader should seek the services of a qualified professional for such advice; the author, publisher, and Bloomberg L.P. cannot be held responsible for any loss incurred as a result of specific health care decisions made by the reader.

First edition published 1998
1 3 5 7 9 10 8 6 4 2

Spragins, Ellyn, 1953–

    Choosing and using an HMO / Ellyn Spragins.

        p.   cm. – (Bloomberg personal bookshelf)

    Includes index.

    ISBN 1-57660-010-6 (alk. paper)

    1. Health maintenance organizations–Evaluation. 2. Health maintenance organizations–Utilization. I. Title. II. Series.

RA413.S67 1997   97-33612

362.1′ 04258—dc21   CIP

Illustrations by Adam McCauley.

Acquired and edited by Christine Miles

Book design by Don Morris Design

For Keenan and Tucker

Live well, my loves.

— E.S.

INTRODUCTION **1**

CHAPTER **1**

The Hunt for Quality

*Cost and convenience count, but quality of care
is what keeps you happy. Here's how to find it* **8**

CHAPTER **2**

The Eleven Indicators of Excellence

*To distill a huge array of information,
concentrate on these measures of superiority* **30**

CHAPTER **3**

Digging Deeper

*After you find the "best" HMOs, see if their
specific strengths match your needs* **52**

CHAPTER **4**

Special Care: Chronically Ill and Seniors

*If your demands are constant and focus on
prevention, the search gets tougher* **98**

CHAPTER 5

Who's the Best Doctor?

*Word of mouth is not enough. Here's help for checking out
certifications, credentials, and complaints* **128**

CHAPTER 6

Getting the Most Out of Your Plan

*What strategies can you use when you feel
thwarted by your HMO?* **158**

CHAPTER 7

Challenging Your HMO

*Getting the most out of Medicare HMOs
and legal remedies* **182**

STATE-BY-STATE
GUIDE TO THE
BEST HMOs **210**

INDEX **246**

ACKNOWLEDGMENTS

I OWE MANY PEOPLE for their generous help. I'm especially grateful to David Lansky, Sue Sheffler, Dwight McNeill, and Diane Archer for their expertise and thoughtfulness. Bruce Bradley at General Motors, a much-needed agent for change, shared his company's abundant research. Other organizations whose research strengthened this book in many ways: the National Committee for Quality Assurance, HCIA Inc., the American Medical Association, the American Association of Health Plans, the Center for the Study of Services, and GTE.

I'd also like to thank Hank Gilman and the editors at *Newsweek* who supported my interest in examining quality differences among HMOs. Chris Miles, my editor, shepherded me through this project with a perfect blend of patience, kindness, and wisdom. My friends Dotty, Jill, Wally, Katie, and Lindsay were all ears even when my message got boring and insisted on lunch therapy when necessary. My father and siblings indulged me with countless pats on the back. Thanks Dad, Betsy, Chuck, Jodi, and Cricket. And I must thank John, my great husband, for his unflagging confidence in me.

INTRODUCTION

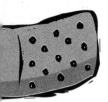

"WHAT IF . . . you didn't have to worry about health care?"

That's the question plastered across a pale blue billboard next to Interstate 95. It's meant to be an advertisement for Blue Cross Blue Shield of New Jersey. But when I drive by this massive sign it strikes me as a dismal commentary on how vastly health care has changed in the past five years and how threatened we feel by those changes. We do worry about health care now. We didn't used to.

There are lots of fascinating books about the future of health care in this country, but this isn't one of them. This book has just one purpose: to give you the tools for selecting and getting the most out of a health plan. HMO executives have told me that consumers don't really care about the quality of health care. They care about adequate parking and whether their doctor is in an HMO's network. I think that's pure arrogance. We care tremendously, but we don't know how to judge quality. We don't have the vocabulary or the yardsticks. And we certainly don't have the information we need from HMO executives. Does your HMO tell you which of its doctors has the best record with pediatric asthma or rehabilitating heart attack victims? Does its marketing brochure tell you how many members' chronic conditions deteriorated or how many died from different diseases?

By learning how to recognize good quality health plans you will accomplish two very important things. First, you'll begin the process of becoming a smart, self-directed, health care consumer. Medical consumerism is in its infancy now. But it will become increasingly important as our population ages and grows more vulnerable to illness and as our employers and government ask us to shoulder more responsibility for our health. Becoming more knowledgeable, more assertive, and more demanding about getting good health care will benefit you and your family for decades to come.

The second benefit of knowing a good health plan when you see one: You can send a powerful message to the health care industry. Right now corporations are an HMO's key customer. And they care more about the size of their health care bills than obtaining the best health care quality possible for employees. So HMOs focus intensely on keeping costs down, even if it means skimping on medical services. In fact, HMOs that do the best job at pinching pennies win the most business and can grow the fastest. The way to break this cost-driven cycle? High-caliber HMOs have to be rewarded for their quality. The only way that can happen is if you and thousands of other consumers pick the best quality plan among the ones offered to you and your spouse—or if you demand better options from your employer. When you start seeing billboards that tout an HMO's audited statistics rather than an image that plays off our fears, you'll know that your message is getting through.

CHAPTER

1

The Hunt
FOR QUALITY

IMAGINE A WORLD in which each corporation has its own accounting rules. All companies track revenue, expenses, and profits—in order to operate their businesses—but each one defines those terms differently. If you want to know whether Company A is more profitable than Company B, you're stuck. The net income of one simply can't be compared with the other.

This confusing situation is exactly the state of affairs among HMOs today. Instead of accounting rules, however, it's quality measures that are being defined differently by every organization. Why? Though a handful of HMOs have been around for decades, the industry is young and changing fast. It hasn't had much time to agree on what, exactly, high quality health care is. A mutual fund's performance is easily summarized by its annual total return. You can judge a car on its

horsepower, gas mileage, or safety record. But it's incredibly difficult to boil down health care quality to a few simple numbers. Is it the percentage of children in a plan who were fully immunized last year? Or is it the number of enrollees who died from heart disease? HMOs, the large employers who contract with them, consumer advocate groups, and the government are still in the process of figuring out the answers to those questions.

One giant obstacle to measuring quality: HMO members' health varies enormously. HIP of Greater New York is one of the most experienced health plans in the metropolitan area. But it has a large proportion of poorer and older inner-city enrollees who are far more susceptible to certain illnesses than an "ordinary" population. Medicaid members, for example, represent 10 percent of all HIP enrollees, but account for 23 percent of the plan's hospital admissions for asthmatic emergencies. And the plan's 65-and-older members comprise 9 percent of HIP's enrollment, but are involved in 54 percent of HIP's congestive heart failures. In contrast, Oxford Health Plans, another New York–based HMO, has only 4.7 percent Medicaid and 6.7 percent Medicare enrollees. So it's no surprise HIP's adult admissions for asthma were nearly twice as high as Oxford's in 1995. Adjusting for such dramatic variances among HMO members is obviously critical—but no one is certain how to do it yet.

Despite those uncertainties, it's absolutely critical that consumers begin demanding superior quality from their HMOs. Right now the No. 1 force driving most HMOs is profit, not quality. That's why the industry is jammed with entrepreneurs and multimillion-dollar mergers. "People have to be alarmed that all these decisions are being made for money," says Dwight McNeill, president of WayPoint Health in Barrington, Rhode Island. "Wall Street has made a bundle. The rest of us pray that we'll never get sick." On a more personal level, seeking out high quality in an HMO is likely to make you happier in the long run. Most people choose an HMO on the basis of cost and convenience, according to Todd Cooperman, president of CareData Reports Inc., a New York–based company that surveys consumers. But they choose to leave because they're unhappy with customer service or the quality of care they're getting.

Assessing how well an HMO will take care of you

and your family is extremely tough. There's no short-cut. You need to look at each plan's quality measures, but also recognize its shortcomings. You need to know what the results of satisfaction surveys really mean. You need to know where to go to find independent analysis of HMO quality. It's not only up to you to put together the pieces of the puzzle, it's imperative that you do so. Here's how to locate the yardsticks for measuring the quality of an HMO's care.

DO look for HMOs with NCQA accreditation.

WOULDN'T IT BE NICE IF someone could make our lives easier by just slapping a Good Housekeeping Seal of Approval on the best HMOs? Actually, someone is: the National Committee for Quality Assurance. A not-for-profit based in Washington, D.C., the NCQA was formed in 1979 by the Group Health Association of America, a trade association for the managed care trade industry (now known as the American Association of Health Plans). Now an independent entity, NCQA has been enormously successful at spurring HMOs to focus on quality in two ways. First, it formulated and pushed for the adoption of common standards for measuring quality. Second, in 1991 it began investigating and reviewing HMOs for accreditation. These accomplishments represent giant steps forward for consumers. Now, at last, you can reasonably compare plans that have been accredited by the NCQA. And, you can be confident that a NCQA-accredited HMO is being scrutinized by an independent third party.

So why isn't picking an excellent HMO as easy as choosing one that's received NCQA accreditation? Much of what NCQA has been examining has more to do with an HMO's organizational prowess—not its ability to make its members healthier. "The accreditation process is very demanding, but it often feels like a ridiculous exercise," explains David Lansky, president of the Foundation for Accountability, a Portland, Oregon, group that is developing new measures of HMO quality. To get accredited, for example, HMOs are asked to document committee meetings on quality, keep their medical records neatly, and count the number of mammograms they execute, among other things. Taking mammograms is important, points out Lansky, but "the HMO's radiologists could be throwing away films as fast as they are taking them." The real question: are more women surviving breast cancer?

Still, an NCQA-accredited HMO is worth seeking, for two reasons. First, an HMO that has sought and received the NCQA's okay is willing to be judged. That doesn't prove a plan's quality will steadily improve, but it shows a willingness to meet certain standards. Obviously, that's the philosophy all of us would like our HMOs to have. Second, NCQA accreditation will help you compare one plan to another as well as match an HMO's strengths to your family's needs.

NCQA's other role is also extremely important to consumers. In addition to accrediting plans, the influential organization publishes a set of performance measures that many plans have adopted and now report to the public. As NCQA adds to and updates these yardsticks, they are starting to become more meaningful. Two of the newest measures it supports regarding breast cancer, for example, ask HMOs to report the stage at which breast cancer is detected among its members and the percentage of women who receive appropriate follow-up care after having an abnormal mammogram. As NCQA continues to improve its criteria in this way, its stamp of approval will become more and more meaningful.

In deciding whether or not to award accreditation to an HMO, NCQA grades it on more than 50 standards in six areas of operation: commitment to quality improvement; investigation of doctors' credentials;

attentiveness to its members and to member complaints; emphasis on preventive health services; consistency in denying or providing care; and good record keeping.

Here's what the NCQA's different levels of accreditation mean:

◆ **Full accreditation.** The best of the bunch. Plans that meet NCQA standards and have excellent quality-improvement programs are granted three-year accreditation. About half of the 338 plans that applied by June 1997 made the grade.

◆ **One-year accreditation.** Plans that meet most standards and have established improvement programs are given one-year accreditation. NCQA reviews the HMO after a year to see if it's acted on recommendations and can move up to full accreditation. Thirty-six percent of plans that apply fall into this category.

◆ **Provisional accreditation.** These HMOs have a way to go. Though they may have quality improvement programs and meet some of the NCQA's standards, they "need to demonstrate progress before they can qualify for higher levels of accreditation," says Ann Greiner, an assistant vice president at NCQA. The number of HMOs with this barely passing grade: 16, or 6 percent.

◆ **Denial.** Sixteen plans flunked the NCQA's review altogether in mid-1997 (see "Accreditation Flunkees," pgs. 16–17).

◆ **Under review.** This is a sign of a plan's discontent. The NCQA gave these plans an accreditation grade, but they've asked the grade to be reviewed. Seven plans which had applied for accreditation were under review in mid-1997.

◆ **Discretionary review.** These plans are raising questions at NCQA. The group accredited a plan, but later decided to revisit its decision.

ACCREDITATION FLUNKEES

NOT EVERY HMO THAT'S DENIED NCQA accreditation should be shunned. For example, Providence Good Health Plan in Portland, Oregon, was denied accreditation from the NCQA in 1996. Why? It delegated the credentialing of its doctors to hospitals instead of doing it itself. Yet the plan is considered top-notch by experts and won GTE's "exceptional" designation because its quality is so high.

Still, it's probably smart to avoid plans that have flunked. It sends an important message about how much you value the quality of your health care and, more importantly, it's likely to safeguard your family's health. You can ask the NCQA for a free accreditation list (800-839-6487), or look it up on the Web site (www.ncqa.org). Here's a list of the HMOs which had been denied accreditation as of March 1996:

◆ Aetna Health Plans of California—Los Angeles market (Loma Linda, CA)
◆ Aetna Health Plans of San Diego (San Diego, CA)
◆ CaliforniaCare (Woodland Hills, CA)
◆ Capital District Physicians' Health (Albany, NY)
◆ CareNetwork, Inc. (Milwaukee, WI)
◆ Complete Health, Inc. (Birmingham, AL)
◆ Emphesys Wisconsin Insurance Co. (Green Bay, WI)

DON'T forget the details.

WHILE IT'S TEMPTING TO simply pick a plan with full accreditation, which NCQA gives to the highest-scoring HMOs, looking beyond the surface is paramount to making a good choice among HMOs. A first step: the NCQA's two-page Accreditation Summary Reports, which are available for $3.00 each from NCQA (800-839-6487) or free on NCQA's Web site (www.ncqa.org). While the reports unfortunately divulge only a few pieces of the nitty-gritty behind a

- Foundation Health, South Florida (Miami, FL)
- Health Plan of Nevada, Inc. (Las Vegas, NV)
- Healthplan Southeast (Tallahassee, FL)
- Heritage National Healthplan, Inc. (Moline, IL)
- Humana Medical Plan, Inc. (Jacksonville, FL)
- Independent Health (Buffalo, NY)
- Independent Health-Hudson Valley (Tarrytown, NY)
- Medical Value Plan (Toledo, OH)
- Mid Atlantic Medical Services, Inc.: MD-IPA and Optimum Choice, Inc. (Rockville, MD)
- NYLCare Health Plan (Houston, TX)
- PacifiCare of Oklahoma (Tulsa, OK)
- Pasteur Health Plan HMO (Hialeah, FL)
- PCA/Century Medical Health Plan of Florida—Central Region (Orlando, FL)
- PCA/Century Medical Health Plan of Florida—South Region (Miami, FL)
- PCA/Century Medical Health Plans of Florida—North Region (Jacksonville, FL)
- Providence Health Plans (Seattle, WA)
- Total Health Care (Kansas City, MO)
- United Health Plan (Inglewood, CA)
- United Physicians Health Network (Evansville, IN)

plan's accreditation level, they can help you compare one HMO to another in a very broad way.

First, consider a plan's age and organizational mandate, described on the report's first page. I'm biased toward long-established, not-for-profit plans even though studies have shown that not-for-profits aren't necessarily more effective or caring than for-profit plans. Why? Simple. Not-for-profits consistently dominate the lists of top-rated HMOs. Among the 23 HMOs to win GTE's "Exceptional Quality Designation" *(see GTE's 1997 list, pg. 19)*, many are not-for-profits such as Harvard Pilgrim Health Care in Boston, Massachusetts; Pellon Community Health Plan in Worcester, Massachusetts; Scott and White Health Plan in Temple, Texas; and Kaiser's Northwest, Georgia, North Carolina, and Mid-Atlantic plans. Kaiser's California and Colorado plans, which are the oldest HMOs in the country, ranked high on the lists in both *Consumer Reports* and *U.S. News & World Report,* as well as on the annual scorecard that I conduct for *Newsweek.* In truth, it's not their not-for-profit status that makes these blue-chip HMOs standard-bearers. It's that they prize close, collaborative relationships with their doctors and have decades of experience in improving people's health. In the simplest sense, they've worked out many of the kinks in managed care.

Next, look at the six charts on the report's second page. These tell you how a plan stacked up against the competition in six key areas that the NCQA scrutinizes. If you're comparing two plans against each other, the one with the highest scores (as measured by performance levels of "Minimal," "Partial," "Significant," or "Full") is obviously preferable. If there are areas of weakness, where one plan scores lower than the other or lower than the average health plan, look at how important that category is to you. The NCQA itself assigns a lower weighting to four areas: preventive health, the completeness of medical records, the approval process for medical care, and the responsiveness to member needs.

If a member of your family is chronically sick or needs frequent consultations with specialists, for example, you should look for an HMO with a very high score in "utilization management," the category involving how quickly and fairly the plan makes decisions about treatment.

GTE'S EXCEPTIONAL QUALITY PLANS

◆ Blue Care Network–Health Central (Lansing, MI)
◆ Fallon Community Health Plan (Worcester, MA)
◆ FPH Colorado, Inc. (Colorado Springs, CO)
◆ Group Health Cooperative (Eau Claire, WI)
◆ Group Health Cooperative of Puget Sound (Seattle, WA)
◆ Group Health Northwest (Spokane, WA)
◆ Harvard Pilgrim Health Plan (Boston, MA)
◆ Health Partners (Minneapolis, MN)
◆ Health Plus–WA (Mountlake Terrace, WA)
◆ Kaiser Foundation Health Plan of Georgia (Atlanta, GA)
◆ Kaiser Foundation Health Plan–Hawaii Region (Honolulu, HI)
◆ Kaiser Foundation Health Plan of Mid-Atlantic States (Washington, DC)
◆ Kaiser Permanente–Northeast Region (Stamford, CT)
◆ Kaiser Permanente Health Plan of North Carolina (Raleigh/Durham, NC)
◆ Kaiser Foundation Health Plan of the Northwest (Portland, OR)
◆ Kaiser Foundation Health Plan of Northern California (San Francisco, CA)
◆ Kaiser Foundation Health Plan of Southern California (Los Angeles, CA)
◆ Lifeguard (San Francisco, CA)
◆ Matthew Thornton Health Plan (Nashua, NH)
◆ Physicians Plus (Madison, WI)
◆ Providence Good Health Plan of Oregon (Portland, OR)
◆ Scott and White Health Plan (Temple, TX)
◆ Tufts Health Plan (Boston, MA)

DO get hard data.

THE NCQA'S REPORTS WILL GIVE you an overview of an HMO's strengths and weaknesses, but what you really need to make an excellent choice are the myriad details that make up a health plan. Here's why. Look at two health plans that operate in northern California: Aetna Health Plans of California, Inc., and Kaiser Foundation Health Plan, Inc. The first, a national for-profit company with HMOs in more than 20 markets, has had full accreditation from the NCQA since 1993. Until recently Kaiser, a 60-year-old not-for-profit, did not yet have accreditation. The right choice seems easy enough: Aetna, the plan that has been accredited longer.

A closer look might change your mind, however. One of the simplest and most basic activities that HMOs engage in is preventive health, such as immunizing children and screening for breast and cervical cancer. Aetna in 1994 administered the appropriate vaccines to 70.8 percent of the children in its plan. That's a reasonably good performance compared to the average California HMO, which immunized only 72.2 percent. But it's far below Kaiser's achievement: 85.5 percent. Similarly, Aetna accomplished far less in screening for breast and cervical cancer, reaching only 58.4 percent and 54 percent of members compared to Kaiser's 73.5 percent and 76 percent.

This is the level of detail that will help you separate one HMO from another in a meaningful way—and match an HMO's strengths to your family's needs. You can find this fine-grained data in something called HEDIS, which stands for Health Plan Employer Data and Information Set (because the measures were originally developed for the large companies that hire HMOs). It contains 60 measures that cover everything from a plan's immunization rates to the loyalty of its members to the availability of its mental health services. Hundreds of plans have been reporting on their own performance, using HEDIS as a common yard-stick, since the early 1990s. And starting in 1997, many of them began using an even more comprehensive version of HEDIS.

There are three ways to get HEDIS information on a health plan: directly from the plan itself, from your employer's benefits department, or through an NCQA database called Quality Compass (800-839-6487). Quality Compass offers a key advantage that the others don't: perspective on a plan's perfor-mance. Each performance score can be compared to a regional and national average as well as to a bench-mark. So, for example, Quality Compass will tell you that Cigna of Florida, in southern Florida, admitted 1.84 percent of children with asthma attacks to the hospital in 1995. In contrast, other HMOs in the region admitted 3.15 percent while HMOs across the country hospitalized 2.94 percent.

The major drawback to Quality Compass is that it's expensive. A paper report or CD-ROM covering one to 25 plans costs $800. The best alternative to buying it yourself is to find out if your employer or a local library has purchased it. If they haven't, consider get-ting the data directly from the plan and comparing it to the Eleven Leading Indicators of Excellence listed on pages 34–35.

The second drawback: HEDIS is far from perfect. That's why United HealthCare Corp., which operates more than 40 plans with 14 million enrollees, was unwilling to directly answer the questions that I sub-mitted for *Newsweek*'s 1996 survey of HMO quality. "Although HEDIS offers a wealth of information, it also should be viewed as a work in progress," explains Diana Campau, a company spokesperson. Similarly Humana, which owns 23 HMOs covering three mil-lion people, believes the HEDIS measures are flawed and easily misunderstood by consumers. What's more, most of the HEDIS data being published by the plans and NCQA hasn't been audited. There's no way to be sure that the plans are measuring themselves with the exacting technical methods demanded by HEDIS.

Still, HEDIS is by far the most advanced and widespread set of criteria that exists for HMOs. Any plan that isn't reporting HEDIS data—despite its shortcomings—isn't doing enough to let consumers evaluate its effectiveness in treating sick and healthy members. That's reason enough to cross a plan off your list.

DON'T ignore trends.

HMOS CAN BE ON THEIR way up—or down—the quality ladder. The key things that can hurt HMO quality have to do with growth. The effort to coordinate and standardize care in two different organizations after a merger can seriously detract from an HMO's service and quality. Similarly, a rapidly expanding HMO which is signing up hundreds or thousands of new doctors can't honestly say that its care is consistently high—or even that it's consistent at all. That's why it's critical to look at more than one year's quality measures in evaluating an HMO's quality.

Consider NYLCare Health Plan of the Gulf Coast, a Houston-based HMO that I rated "satisfactory"—the lowest possible grade—in *Newsweek*'s 1996 ranking of 43 HMOs. Alphabetization of the list also pushed NYLCare to the very bottom of the list. It looked like an HMO to avoid. In fact, while you might not pick NYLCare over Harris Methodist Health Plan, in Arlington, Texas, because its quality and service scores were not as high, you might at least consider it if you were to review at least two years of quality statistics. For example, in 1994 NYLCare was denied accreditation from NCQA. Between 1995 and 1996, however, the plan began making progress. The percentage of pregnant members receiving early prenatal care rose from 85 to 90 percent and the proportion of heart attack victims receiving beta blockers, a highly effective drug, jumped from 48 percent to 61 percent. "In the early 1990s we were growing for growth's sake," says Mike Mirt, NYLCare's president. "But in 1993 we embraced the goal of becoming a quality organization and now we're beginning to see the results of those efforts."

DO look at other accrediting bodies.

WHILE NCQA IS BY FAR the most visible accrediting organization, it's not the only game in town. Here's a description of the other three:

◆ **The Joint Commission on Accreditation of Healthcare Organizations (JCAHO).** Founded in 1951, the not-for-profit JCAHO is an old hand at health care accreditation, but its focus has long been hospitals and other organizations. It's evaluated and accredited nearly 5,300 hospitals and over 9,000 home care, long term care, behavioral health care, laboratory and ambulatory care companies. In 1994 it began an accreditation program for HMOs and managed care network plans and, at the same time, began planning to incorporate tougher outcomes measures into all of its accreditation process. So far, it's accredited 19 managed care organizations.

Accreditation from the Oakbrook Terrace, Illinois, organization means that a hospital, plan, or health care service must undergo an onsite survey by a joint commission team at least every three years. Surveyors also visit sites where enrollees actually receive their care. Here are the seven standards that plans are judged on: how a plan addresses ethical issues; the continuity and spectrum of care available; a plan's efforts to educate its members; initiative in creating better care; management of staff; use of performance information; and plans for improving performance. Once JCAHO has accredited a critical mass of plans, you'll be able to order a free performance report which shows how a plan fared in these areas and how it scored compared to its peers. Call JCAHO at 630-792-5800, or check JCAHO's Web site (www.jcaho.org) in early 1998.

◆ **Medical Quality Commission.** Another not-for-profit, the Medical Quality Commission was founded just six years ago and is based in Seal Beach, California. It accredits not HMOs, but doctor group practices and independent physician associations. To win three-year accreditation groups must meet 150 criteria in 14 areas of review. So far only 30 groups have been accredited. Though only 3 percent of the groups that apply for accreditation don't win it, the low fail rate doesn't mean that obtaining accreditation from the commission is a snap. "There's no economic incentive from the marketplace for groups that are accredited by us. So, only groups that are extremely motivated to succeed apply," explains Lori Bloomfield, the commission's chief operating officer. Call 310-936-1100 for a list of accredited groups. The commission can also give you the results of a patient satisfaction survey of 55 doctors' groups in California, Oregon, and Washington. The report will let you see how a group scored in seven different areas, and is also available on the commission's Web site (www.tmqc.org).

◆ **American Accreditation HealthCare Commission/URAC.** The focus of this group has traditionally been utilization review, which is industry jargon for keeping an eye on how many services doctors and hospitals provide to members. An overly tough UR process means providers get their hands slapped by the health plan when they provide too many services. So far 150 preferred provider networks, physician-hospital organizations, and other health networks have had their UR programs accredited.

DON'T be satisfied with most satisfaction survey reports.

PEOPLE FEEL THEY'RE really getting the lowdown on an HMO when they can find out how members rated it in a satisfaction survey. Members, after all, don't have any reason to lie about how happy—or unhappy—they are with their HMO. Instead of judging a health plan on the basis of a neighbor's or a colleague's opinion, you get to review the collective wisdom of people like you.

The trouble is, satisfaction surveys aren't always what they seem. HMOs first began asking members about how happy they were only a few years ago. Why? Not because the health plans' managers wanted to know. The HMOs were simply responding to requests by corporations, which were trying to select an HMO for employees. While most HMOs now regularly query their members, there's little incentive to tell you, the public, anything unfavorable. And much of what health plans do report, in advertisements or brochures, can be easily manipulated to make the HMO look good.

The most common of such data-burnishing techniques: lumping together several levels of satisfied customers. HMOs typically ask members to score their approval on a one-through-five scale, with five representing the highest level of satisfaction. Instead of reporting how it fared in each category, though, HMOs will often add together the percentage of members who gave it a three or higher. Then it can claim, as HIP of Greater New York does in its 1994 report on quality, that 80 percent of its members were satisfied with the plan. A footnote reveals that HIP pooled members whose satisfaction rating was "good" with members who rated the HMO as "excellent" and "very good" to come up with that 80 percent figure.

A key lesson: examine the highest and lowest ratings of an HMO's satisfaction survey. According to

CareData Reports, satisfaction levels for HMOs in the same region can vary dramatically. Members who were extremely or very dissatisfied with five New York HMOs—HIP, Kaiser, Oxford, Vytra, and U.S. Health-care—ranged from 2 percent to 14 percent in 1994. At the other end of the spectrum, Oxford had the largest share of happy customers—26 percent said they were extremely satisfied—while HIP had the smallest, with only 10 percent reporting the highest level of satisfaction. Also make sure that you're looking at satisfaction levels of a regional plan, as opposed to a large national company. The aggregated scores for Aetna's or Cigna's health plans across the country are meaningless because you're only going to get your health care from one of them.

Don't make the mistake of believing that stellar satisfaction levels mean a plan is delivering high quality care. Believe it or not, the two often don't go hand in hand. In a 1996 study of 17 HMOs, the Massachusetts Healthcare Purchaser Group, a coalition of government and corporations, discovered that the HMOs with the highest quality score were not the ones with the highest satisfaction scores. How can that be? When you ask members about their satisfaction levels, you're finding out about perceptions, not clinical outcomes. So courteous, helpful phone reps and the ability to get an appointment within 24 hours can win a plan a top satisfaction rating, even if it's doing a lousy job of keeping members healthy.

The Massachusetts study showed how dangerous picking HMOs on the basis of satisfaction scores could be. U.S. Healthcare earned one of the highest overall satisfaction ratings—four stars. But it performed miserably on the quality indicators, with one of the lowest scores among the 17 plans. Harvard Community Health Plan (later merged with Pilgrim to become Harvard Pilgrim Health Plan), Fallon, and Kaiser clinched the highest quality spots while Tufts and

Healthsource won the highest satisfaction ratings.

So, should you simply ignore satisfaction ratings in your hunt for quality? No, but understand their limitations. They can give you a preview of how it will feel to deal with an HMO and help you match an HMO's service abilities to your family's needs, but they won't give you a clue about the true quality of its care.

You can find satisfaction data in a number of places: the latest version of HEDIS (3.0) contains a satisfaction survey which hundreds of plans have begun using. The single largest source of this information is

SACHS/SCARBOROUGH'S CHAMPIONS

IN 1994 SACHS GROUP, a health care information company in Evanston, Illinois, and Scarborough Research, a market research organization in New York, New York, decided to yoke their expertise and survey consumers about their satisfaction with HMOs. After surveying 85,000 consumers in 27 U.S. markets, it anointed nine health plans to the Sachs Honor Roll. To make the list below, the HMOs had to rate significantly higher than other plans in their market on 24 satisfaction measures.

◆ ChoiceCare Health Plans, Inc. (Cincinnati, OH)
◆ Harris Methodist Health Plan (Dallas/Ft. Worth, TX)
◆ Independence Blue Cross (Philadelphia, PA)
◆ Kaiser Permanente (Atlanta, GA)
◆ Kaiser Permanente (Sacramento, San Francisco, San Diego, Los Angeles, CA)
◆ Kaiser Permanente (Washington, DC)
◆ M-Plan (Indianapolis, IN)
◆ Oxford Health Plans, Inc. (New York, NY)
◆ Physicians Health Services, Inc. (New York, NY)
◆ Prudential HealthCare (Orlando, FL)
◆ Tufts Health Plan (Boston, MA)
◆ United HealthCare of Texas, Inc. (Houston, TX)
◆ United HealthCare of the Midwest, Inc. (St. Louis, MO)

in NCQA's Quality Compass. The surveys aren't audited, but at least they're comparable to each other. A cheaper route is to ask a health plan for its HEDIS 3.0 data, or just the satisfaction survey component. If a plan substitutes its own survey, take it with a grain of salt. You may still learn something from it, but it probably hasn't escaped without a bit of massaging from the HMO's marketing department.

Any HMO that hews to the satisfaction survey contained in HEDIS 3.0 is unlikely to manipulate the numbers to present itself in a better light, but it can always withhold the results of portions of the survey. If you want to get an alternative, unbiased view of how satisfied HMO members are, look in *Checkbook's Guide To Health Insurance Plans For Federal Employees,* published by the Center for the Study of Services in Washington, D.C. The book rates every health insurance plan—more than 400—available to Federal employees in the U.S. In addition to receiving an overall satisfaction score, plans are rated on 21 other satisfaction items ranging from the advice given over the phone to the choice of specialists. In Wisconsin, for example, you can see that Group Health Co-op/SCWisconsin had the highest percentage of members that were extremely satisfied, overall, in 1995. But members were more dissatisfied with their ability to get an appointment for a checkup at this plan than members at most other HMOs in the state.

The book also has an extremely useful section on costs and special features. Here you can see that Group Health Co-op's high satisfaction levels come at a price—both its Madison and Eau Claire plans are relatively expensive compared to their competitors. This section yields another important nugget of information: the "quit" rate. Only 4 percent of Madison's members decided to leave the plan, while 22 percent of Eau Claire's members did. It could be that a large employer decided to drop the Eau Claire plan for reasons that have nothing to do with quality. But still, a high quit rate is the kind of red flag that should prompt you to investigate further before joining a plan. The guide can be purchased for $10.45 by calling 202-347-7283.

CHAPTER

The Eleven
INDICATORS OF
Excellence

SUPPOSE YOU HUNT DOWN all the quality measures that exist for the plans you have to choose among. Now you've got a huge array of information in front of you. How do you compare the HMOs? You could create a grid the size of a football field and pick the HMO with the highest scores in the greatest number of categories. If you have the patience for it, this approach has several advantages. It will acquaint you with every nook and cranny of the HMOs you're considering, and it will likely net you a fine health plan.

But there are some drawbacks to this technique. It's incredibly tedious. And the extra effort may not help you make the best choice. Why? Because each piece of the quality puzzle is not equally valid. HEDIS measures, for example, are based on information that is famously

unreliable. The California Cooperative Healthcare Reporting Initiative, a not-for-profit business
coalition in San Francisco, found that many
doctors were simply not recording the procedures, screenings, and other treatments that
are crucial to calculating a health plan's
mammography rate, for example, or its immunization rate. So it finally abandoned the idea
of using HEDIS data, and now tracks down 33,000
patient charts each year in order to generate

its own measures, which it publishes in an annual report card. Unlike the HEDIS numbers, CCHRI's figures have been audited. "They're numbers you can believe in," says David Hopkins, a director at the Pacific Business Group on Health.

So how do you choose an HMO? I'd suggest two practical approaches—one described in this chapter and the other in Chapter 3. Instead of analyzing a laundry list of measures, judge your HMO candidates against a select set of measures that signify superiority. Included in the Eleven Leading Indicators of Excellence, *below,* are some HEDIS yardsticks. They may not be as reliable as they should be, as CCHRI discovered, but they are at least a rough gauge of key areas that should be scrutinized. Complementing those measures are a handful of other characteristics commonly found in top performing plans.

ELEVEN LEADING INDICATORS OF EXCELLENCE

A QUICK AND REASONABLY comprehensive way to judge an HMO's quality of care is to see how many of the leading indicators of excellence it has.

1 A 15- to 20-year history—This operating experience should be in your region.

2 Full accreditation and reporting on FACCT (Foundation for Accountability) measures—The highest level of accreditation from the National Committee for Quality Assurance and plans to use quality measures from the Foundation for Accountability.

3 Not-for-profit status with doctors on staff or in a group—Financial considerations shouldn't rule.

4 Low heart bypass and angioplasty rates—1.5 bypasses per thousand men between the ages of 45 and 64 and 1.6 angioplasties per thousand men in the same age group.

5 Relatively few Caesarean sections—15 percent or less of all childbirths.

Each of the 11 indicators was designed to carry a lot of freight. Rather than telling you merely how successful the health plan is in accomplishing a single procedure, an indicator is meant to speak volumes about entire chunks of an HMO's care. For example, an ideal indicator would be the percentage of women in a health plan who deliver children vaginally after having previously had a Caesarean section, called the "VBAC" rate.

Why is a high VBAC rate a mark of excellence? First, it tells you that the HMO knows that such delivery is possible for many women, a fact that has not been widely understood, even by doctors. Second, it tells you that the HMO recognizes that such VBAC deliveries are far safer than surgery for their members. Third, the rate signifies that the HMO has been able to actually change its doctors' practice habits so as to

6 High cervical and breast cancer screening rates—at least 85 percent of all women members between the ages of 52 and 64 have had a mammogram during the prior two years, and at least 85 percent of all women between the ages of 21 and 64 have had a Pap test during the preceding three years.

7 High diabetic retinal testing rates—at least 64 percent of the appropriate diabetic population.

8 Excellent follow-up after hospitalization for a mental disorder—96 percent or more of discharged members are followed-up.

9 Available doctors—at least 90 percent of doctors should be accepting new patients.

10 Highly satisfied doctors—doctor's turnover should be less than 10 percent.

11 Highly satisfied members—65 percent to 75 percent or more of members are "completely satisfied," and "very satisfied."

encourage VBACs where possible—no mean feat. Finally, because it takes some effort and insight to know which women are good candidates for VBACs, the rate shows you that an HMO has enough accurate and well-organized information to be able to spot those women. These are all hallmarks of what managed care at its best can accomplish, in contrast to the old fee-for-service system.

Unfortunately, most HMOs can't tell you their VBAC rates, but there are other measures that offer comparable pictures. The 11 leading indicators previously listed aren't failproof. But HMOs that score most highly on these measures, such as Fallon Community Health Plan, in Worcester, Massachusetts, and Harvard Pilgrim Health Plan, in Boston, Massachusetts, are delivering the best care in the country. Most of the yardsticks calling for a certain rate—such as the percentage of women who have received mammograms—are HEDIS measures published by health plans or available in Quality Compass, a database maintained by the National Committee for Quality Assurance. You'll find the other measures where noted.

If you decide to choose your HMO using this method, remember that each "indicator" carries extra significance. Don't omit any if you can help it. And try to assemble at least two years' worth of figures so that you can get a feel for an HMO's direction. To find an excellent HMO:

DO look for a 15- to 20-year history.

AGE IS NOT A VIRTUE by itself. But 15 to 20 years of maturation in your region of the country enables an organization to figure out a few things, including how to pay and retain good doctors and hospitals. An HMO that has solid relations with those front-line providers can usually deliver better and more coordinated care than an HMO that has just begun working with its doctors and hospitals. Ask your employer or the HMO itself for its corporate history. Watch for any recent mergers or conversions from not-for-profit to for-profit status. At best they strain an organization's operations. At worst they can disrupt—or completely sever—relations with doctors and hospitals.

DON'T go with a for-profit HMO and doctors with financial risk.

EXPERTS ARGUE ENDLESSLY about whether money plays a role in the quality of care that health plans deliver. Of course it does! The opportunity to make more money by refusing or stinting on a patient's care pops up in two places—the doctor's office and the HMO's executive offices. Doctors who are paid a flat monthly rate to provide care for a group of patients are "capitated." They are often at risk for losing money if they order too many expensive tests or refer members to specialists too frequently. In contrast, staff doctors have no financial incentive to provide too much or too little health care. While most doctors undoubtedly provide the best care they can, no matter how they're compensated, the best HMOs in the country have reached the top of the quality ladder in part because their doctors are employees, truly engaged in delivering care without fear of being personally penalized.

Similarly, a for-profit HMO is dramatically different from a not-for-profit plan. While both have an incentive to keep costs down, the not-for-profits in this country tend to be far more focused on members' well-being. And the for-profits? The most potent symbol of their objective, argues Dwight McNeill, president of WayPoint Health in Barrington, Rhode Island, is that "Lenny Abrahamson sold U.S. Healthcare, the company he founded, to Aetna for $1 billion. If that doesn't say everything about what's driving HMOs, then we're not going to wake up in time." A not-for-

profit isn't by definition better than a beast owned by
Wall Street investors. But so far, it's proven one of the
sturdiest indicators of excellence.

DO demand a fully accredited plan and reporting on FACCT measures.

A PLAN THAT'S ACCREDITED by the National Committee for Quality Assurance is doing a great deal to
improve the quality of its care. But a truly excellent
plan is willing to hold itself up to an even higher standard of quality. The Foundation for Accountability is
a Portland, Oregon, coalition of companies and consumer advocates which has begun formulating new
quality measures that are even tougher than those
being used by HEDIS. FACCT is asking an HMO not
only how successful it has been in keeping breast cancer victims disease-free for five years, for example, but
how the women felt about the information, communication, and services they received during treatment.
Any HMO that is planning to answer such questions is
exemplary—and any that is already doing so is extra-
ordinary. Ask your HMO if it plans to report on
FACCT measures. If it doesn't, ask if it plans to report
HEDIS 3.0 measures, the newest version of standard
HMO yardsticks. Most of the country's plans should
be able to do so in 1997.

DON'T agree to high heart bypass and angioplasty rates.

THE BEST HEALTH PLANS help their members prevent heart disease. For participants who do develop it,
these plans fully exploit treatments such as diet, exercise, or drug therapy before resorting to invasive procedures. But don't look at the percentage of heart
bypass surgeries (called CABG, for cardiac artery
bypass graft) at an HMO without looking also at
angioplasty rates, or the percentage of members
whose arterial plaque is cleared by a tiny balloon

inserted into the vein. A low CABG rate accompanied by a high angioplasty rate doesn't show the excellent prevention and low-risk treatment approach you're shopping for.

What are good rates? GTE, a large company in Stamford, Connecticut, that scrutinizes over 300 HMOs every year on behalf of its employees, has established benchmarks drawn from the experience of the best HMOs it can find. For heart bypasses, the rate is 1.5 per thousand men between the ages of 45 and 64. For angioplasties, it's 1.6 per thousand men in the same age group. How likely are you to find an HMO with rates this low? Not very. The national averages are 4.1 per thousand for bypasses and 4.8 per thousand for angioplasties. Look for a plan with rates that are lower. "A lot of good plans have rates that are somewhere between the national average and GTE's best practice," says Sue Sheffler, a health care consultant based in Arlington, Massachusetts.

DO require high cervical and breast cancer screening rates, and a low C-section rate.

THE VERY CHEAPEST AND easiest way for an HMO to keep its members healthy is to catch diseases early. If an HMO hasn't figured that out and found a way to screen everyone who should be screened, it's not likely it will excel in the tougher tasks—like surgery, disease management, and chronic illnesses. Use GTE's best practice guidelines as your benchmarks: at least 85 percent of all women between the ages of 52 and 64 have had a mammogram during the prior two years, and at least 85 percent of all women between the ages of 21 and 64 have had a Pap test during the preceding three years. The national average is 70 percent for both, but that's much too low. Don't join an HMO that lets so many people fall through the cracks.

DON'T accept a high proportion of Caesarean sections.

EXPERTS SAY THAT THOUSANDS of the 749,463 C-sections performed each year are unnecessary and expose women to needless danger. C-sections involve anesthesia, major surgery, and longer recovery periods with more complications than normal deliveries. You should look for a C-section rate of 15 percent or less of all childbirths. GTE's top HMOs have whittled the rate to 13.7 percent, while the national average is 20.7 percent.

DO seek high diabetic retinal testing rates.

WHY SHOULD THIS MATTER if neither you nor a member of your family has diabetes? It's another case where a very simple test can prevent a very serious development—blindness—among people with diabetes. It's also a terrific indicator of an HMO's organizational prowess, because the diabetic retinal screening rates for most HMOs are shockingly low: nationally, HMOs test only 37 percent of the appropriate diabetic population each year. Top HMOs are screening 64 percent.

DON'T sign up with a plan that skimps on mental illness.

YOU MAY NEVER HAVE HAD an episode of depression or other psychosis. And if you ever do, you probably won't be hospitalized because of it. But an HMO should be scrutinized on this measure for two reasons. First, HMOs have a particularly bad record in dealing with affective disorders. They've clumsily cut off therapy after an arbitrary number of sessions. They've compromised therapists' confidentiality by asking for detailed reports on patients' problems. And they've frequently farmed out the entire mental health component of their care to an independent organization. Second, getting a fix on the quality of an HMO's mental health efforts is tougher than any other medical activity.

So this gauge is, for now, the best indicator of how an HMO handles mental health issues. The question: how many of the HMO's members who have been hospitalized with a mental disorder received a follow-up phone call or had a follow-up appointment within 30 days of their discharge? Believe it or not, the national average is only 75 percent. And the other 25 percent? "No one's checking on whether they're taking their medication or having any adverse reactions," says Sheffler. "It's outrageous not to follow-up." But you don't have to settle for that—the best plans that GTE tracks average a follow-up rate of 96 percent.

DO find a plan with available doctors.

THIS MEASURE MAY NOT SEEM to make sense. But anyone who has dialed a doctor's phone number off of a health plan's list—only to be told that the doctor is no longer accepting new patients—knows what the problem is. An HMO's physician list may be impressively long, but it's meaningless if those doctors don't want to deal with your HMO anymore. The question to ask an HMO: how many of your doctors have "open panels," or are accepting new patients? Opt for an HMO with at least 90 percent open panels.

DON'T join a plan with unhappy doctors.

DOCTORS AREN'T EASY TO PLEASE. And they especially dislike HMOs because of the way the health plans so noisily intrude upon their domain. So if an HMO gets a thumbs-up from doctors it's worth knowing about. There are three ways of evaluating docs' opinions of an HMO. First, ask the HMO for its annual physician turnover rate. If more than 10 percent of an HMO's doctors leave during a year, ask the HMO why. Also consider querying an independent doctor or your state medical society *(see pgs. 42–48)*.

THE INSIDE TRACK: WHEN DOCTORS RATE HMOs

DOCTORS ARE IN THE BEST possible position for judging HMO quality. So how do we find out what they know? Some state and county medical societies, such as the Hillsborough County Medical Association in Tampa, Florida, are surveying their members to find out. Even if the society itself isn't sponsoring a survey, it may know of doctors' groups, such as the Tucson Alliance for Medical Excellence, in Arizona, that are. Here are phone numbers and Web addresses for the medical societies in all 50 states, starting with the national organization:

The American Medical Association
(www.ama-assn.org)   312-464-5000

STATE MEDICAL SOCIETIES
Medical Association of the State of Alabama
19 S. Jackson St., P.O. Box 1900
Montgomery, AL 36102-1900   334-263-6441

Arizona Medical Association
810 W. Bethany Home Rd.
Phoenix, AZ 85013   602-246-8901

Arkansas Medical Society
10 Corporate Hill Dr., Ste. 300
P.O. Box 5776
Little Rock, AR 72215   501-224-8967

California Medical Association
221 Main St., 2nd Fl.
San Francisco, CA 94105   415-541-0900

Colorado Medical Society
7800 E. Dorado Pl.

Englewood, CO 80111-2306   303-779-5455

Connecticut State Medical Society
160 St. Ronan St.
New Haven, CT 06511   203-865-0587

Medical Society of Delaware
1925 Lovering Ave.
Wilmington, DE 19806   302-658-7596

Medical Society of District of Columbia
2215 M Street NW
Washington, DC 20037-2059   202-466-1800

Florida Medical Association
760 Riverside Ave., P.O. Box 2411
Jacksonville, FL 32203   904-356-1571

Medical Association of Georgia
938 Peachtree St. NE
Atlanta, GA 30309   404-876-7535

Guam Medical Society
275 G Farenholt Ave., Ste. 152
Tamuning, GU 96911-3209   (no phone listed)

Hawaii Medical Association
1360 Beretania St., Ste. 100
Honolulu, HI 96814   808-536-7702

Idaho Medical Association
305 W. Jefferson, P.O. Box 2668
Boise, ID 83702   208-344-7888

(continued)

WHEN DOCTORS RATE HMOs

Illinois State Medical Society
20 N. Michigan Ave., Ste. 700
Chicago, IL 60602   312-782-1654

Indiana State Medical Association
322 Canal Walk, Canal Level
Indianapolis, IN 46202-3252   317-261-2060

Iowa Medical Society
1001 Grand Ave. W
Des Moines, IA 50265   515-223-1401

Kansas Medical Society
623 S.W. 10th Ave.
Topeka, KS 66612   913-235-2383

Kentucky Medical Association
301 N. Hurstbourne Pkwy. S, Ste. 200
Louisville, KY 40222-8512   502-426-6200

Louisiana State Medical Society
3501 N. Causeway Blvd., Ste. 800
Metairie, LA 70002-3673   504-832-9815

Maine Medical Association
P.O. Box 190
Manchester, ME 04351-3374   207-622-3374

Medical and Chirugical Faculty of Maryland
1211 Cathedral St.
Baltimore, MD 21201   410-539-0872

Massachusetts Medical Society
1440 Main St.

Waltham, MA 02154   617-893-4610

Michigan Medical Society
120 W. Saginaw
East Lansing, MI 48826-0950   517-337-1351

Minnesota Medical Association
3433 Broadway St. NE, Ste. 300
Minneapolis, MN 55413-1875   612-378-1875

Mississippi State Medical Association
735 Riverside Dr.
Jackson, MS 39202   601-354-5433

Missouri State Medical Association
113 Madison St., P.O. Box 1028
Jefferson City, MO 65102   573-636-5151

Montana Medical Association
2021 11th Ave., Ste. 12
Helena, MT 59601-4890   406-443-4000

Nebraska Medical Association
233 S 13th St., Ste. 1512
Lincoln, NE 68508-2091   402-474-4472

Nevada State Medical Association
3660 Baker Ln., Ste. 101
Reno, NV 89509   702-825-6788

New Hampshire Medical Society
7 N. State St.
Concord, NH 03301-6389   603-224-1909

(continued)

WHEN DOCTORS RATE HMOs

Medical Society of New Jersey
2 Princess Rd.
Lawrenceville, NJ 08648   609-896-1766

New Mexico Medical Society
7770 Jefferson NE, Ste. 400
Albuquerque, NM 87109   505-828-0237

Medical Society of the State of New York
420 Lakeville Rd., P.O. Box 5404
Lake Success, NY 11042-5404   516-488-6100

North Carolina Medical Society
222 N. Person St., P.O. Box 27167
Raleigh, NC 27611-7167   919-833-3836

North Dakota Medical Association
204 West Thayer Ave., P.O. Box 1198
Bismarck, ND 58502-1198   701-223-9475

Ohio State Medical Association
1500 Lake Shore Dr.
Columbus, OH 43204-3891   614-486-2401

Oklahoma State Medical Association
601 N.W. Expy.
Oklahoma City, OK 73118   405-843-9571

Oregon Medical Association
5210 S.W. Corbett St.
Portland, OR 97201   503-226-1555

Pennsylvania Medical Society
777 E. Park Dr.

Harrisburg, PA 17105-8820   717-558-7750

Puerto Rico Medical Association
Avenue Fernandez Juncos 1305, Ste. 9387
Santruce, PR 00908   809-721-6969

Rhode Island Medical Society
106 Francis St.
Providence, RI 02903   401-331-3207

South Carolina Medical Association
3210 Fernan, P.O. Box 11188
Columbia, SC 29211   803-798-6207

South Dakota State Medical Association
1323 S. Minnesota Ave.
Sioux Falls, SD 57105   605-336-1965

Tennessee Medical Association
2301 21st Ave. S, P.O. Box 120909
Nashville, TN 37212-0909   615-385-2100

Texas Medical Association
401 W. 15th St.
Austin, TX 78701-1680   512-370-1300

Utah Medical Association
540 E. 500 South
Salt Lake City, UT 84102   801-355-7477

Vermont State Medical Society
136 Main St., P.O. Box 1457
Montpelier, VT 05601   802-223-7898

(continued)

WHEN DOCTORS RATE HMOs

Virgin Islands Medical Society
P.O. Box 5982
St. Croix, VI 00823   809-778-5305

Medical Society of Virginia
4205 Dover Rd.
Richmond, VA 23221-3267   804-353-2721

Washington State Medical Association
2033 6th Ave., Ste. 1100
Seattle, WA 98121   206-441-9762

West Virginia State Medical Association
4307 MacCorkle Ave. SE, P.O. Box 4106
Charleston, WV 25364   304-925-0342

State Medical Society of Wisconsin
330 E. Lakeside St., P.O. Box 1109
Madison, WI 53701   608-257-6781

Wyoming Medical Society
1920 Evans, P.O. Box 4009
Cheyenne, WY 82003-4009   307-635-2424

A second approach is to ask your HMO if it surveys its physicians about how happy they are with the HMO and, if so, to give you the results. This is a bit of a long shot. Most HMOs consider the results of such surveys proprietary. If they are willing to disclose the results, chances are you'll only get to see the most positive aspects of the doctors' answers. Still, it's worth a try.

Finally, you should skip the HMO's survey if you're lucky enough to live in a region where an independent-minded consumer advocate group or medical association has surveyed physicians about HMO quality. The first place to go is to your state's medical association *(see pgs. 42–48)*. In 1996 the Hillsborough County Medical Association in Tampa, Florida, asked its 800 physician members to rate the quality of their plan's network, the ease of getting medical referrals, and 16 other questions about HMO care. While only 104 doctors responded, a clear picture of the region's best and worst plans emerged. Cigna received the largest share of "excellent" ratings, while AvMed received the poorest ratings across the board.

DO look for highly satisfied members.

YOU SHOULD NEVER USE satisfaction surveys as a stand-in for an evaluation of overall quality, because they rely on members' perceptions, not hard-core data. Nevertheless, satisfaction surveys can give you an excellent picture of how responsive an HMO is in answering the phone, fielding questions, and otherwise supporting its members. Satisfaction surveys also ask members about the quality of care, but you should review members' responses to these questions with a bit of skepticism. Most HMO members are healthy, so they're not in a position to know how well their plan deals with illnesses.

If you're looking at a HEDIS 3.0 satisfaction survey *(see pgs. 27–28)*, look at the responses to three key questions: No. 11, which addresses overall satisfaction with the HMO; No. 13, which asks if you would recommend the plan; and No. 14, which queries members about plans to switch HMOs. The best HMOs will have a high percentage of members who deem themselves "completely satisfied," and a low percentage who are dissatisfied. Shoot for a better-than-average rate of 65 percent to 75 percent for the combined categories of "completely" and "very" satisfied.

When applying these benchmarks, keep in mind that there are large variations in satisfaction from one region of the country to another *(see pg. 50)*.

SATISFIED? IT DEPENDS

CONSUMERS' SATISFACTION with their HMOs varies tremendously. When reviewing an HMO's satisfaction scores, be sure to put them in the right regional context. Here are the percentage of HMO members who described themselves as "highly satisfied" in 12 different markets surveyed by CareData, an HMO researcher in New York City:

Boston	70.8%
Denver	67.0%
New York	63.1%
Milwaukee	61.7%
Detroit	61.1%
Philadelphia	59.9%
Portland, OR	59.7%
Arizona	58.3%
N. California	58.3%
Dallas	56.4%
Atlanta	55.5%
S. Florida	51.9%

Boston, which enjoys a concentration of high-quality HMOs, has the greatest proportion of people—70.8 percent—who say they're highly satisfied with their HMO. In South Florida, according to CareData Reports, only 51.9 percent feel that satisfied. Because the differences are significant, you may want to use a regional benchmark in judging the satisfaction levels of the HMOs you're considering. Beginning in late 1997, NCQA's Quality Compass (800-839-6487) will contain satisfaction information on individual plans, which can be compared to state, regional, and national averages. CareData (800-526-4466 or www.caredata.com) can give you regional data and satisfaction information on individual HMOs for a small charge.

CHAPTER

3

DIGGING
Deeper

S HELPFUL AS the Eleven Leading Indicators of Excellence will be in directing you to a first-rate health plan, they suffer from a major flaw: They're broad and general. But your health needs aren't—in fact, the medical services and products that you and your family will use are very specific. Does it make sense for all of us to pick the same "best" HMO? Of course not. While plans that truly coordinate and manage your care usually have a philosophy and prowess that reaches throughout the organization, no plan will give you the same level of quality across the board. In *Newsweek*'s 1996 "Best HMOs In America," for example, I deemed Blue Cross Blue Shield of Massachusetts's programs for depression and heart disease extremely good and awarded it high scores in those areas. At 70.8 percent, its cervical cancer screening score,

however, was low, and at 21.5 percent its C-section rate was high. Also, the HMO was completely unwilling to report on how satisfied its members were—a secretive attitude that's unhelpful to consumers. No overall score really does a good job of summarizing this HMO's quality.

The answer is to take a second step in choosing your plan: Find the HMO whose strengths match your family's needs. This is an electrifyingly simple idea that is hard to really use for two reasons. Comparative information on plans simply hasn't been available, and most of us don't have a clue how to forecast our medical needs. But now that HMOs are finally spewing out data, it's time to learn how to predict which services we'll use over the next three to five years. It's not as impossible as it seems. Taken together, your age, sex, physical condition, and parents' medical history can tell you a great deal about your body's medical needs over the next few years. Do you have to make assumptions about the future? Yes. Will the forecast be completely accurate? No. This is essentially guesswork—but it's smart guesswork. No one knows for sure how much money they'll save or what their investments will earn, but that doesn't stop responsible folks from making educated guesses. That's what financial planning for retirement is all about. Planning for your health needs should be no different.

The good news is that our chance of getting a serious illness is quite small. Of the billion or so doctors' visits Americans make each year, the majority are for minor problems, preventive screenings, or general checkups. For example, more adults visit the doctor for Pap smear tests and eye exams in 1995 than for any other reason, according to HCIA Inc., a leading health care information company in Baltimore, Maryland. While blurry vision is nothing to laugh about, it hardly ranks among the dread diseases that we often worry about. Other services in heaviest demand might surprise you with their banality: treatment for blisters and other skin conditions, and X-rays.

Whether you'll need simple or sophisticated treatment, you're far more likely to consume certain services at certain ages than others. So you should pick an HMO that excels in the services you and your family are most likely to need. To help assess those needs, I've designed four family or household profiles: Young Families, Middle-Aged Families with Teenagers, Families with Chronic Illness, and Retirees. Using both inpatient and outpatient data from HCIA, I've narrowed down the specific HMO qualities you should seek for each profile. Because Families with Chronic Illness and Retirees are the most intensive users of health care, those profiles will be handled in Chapter 4.

Many families won't fit tidily into these profiles: single-parent families, for example, or single people. The best strategy is to find the profile that comes closest and then eliminate—or add—certain HMO characteristics to reflect your needs. A single mother with teenagers, for example, could simply omit HMO traits important to middle-aged men. A middle-aged couple who are the parents of an infant, rather than of teenagers, should mix the child-oriented recommendations from the first profile with the middle-age traits in the second.

Before the profiles, here are three recommendations to help you customize your HMO search:

DO start by assessing your medical risks.

CHANCES ARE YOU HAVE a pretty good idea if you face a special health risk.Your great Aunt Dotty had breast cancer, perhaps, or your grandfather died of a heart attack. Your first mission in finding an HMO tailored to you is to get a grip on how real those risks are. If breast cancer really does threaten you, that fact will instantly transform your search. You'll push an HMO's record with breast cancer victims to the top of your list of criteria. You'll also want to thoroughly investigate every aspect of breast cancer treatment and support programs offered by your HMO candidates.

There are a number of ways to find out if you have extreme health risks. You'll get a quick answer by filling out and scoring the questionnaire beginning on page 60, which is taken from *LifePlan: Your Own Master Plan for Maintaining Health and Preventing Illness,* by Donald M. Vickery, M.D. (Health Decisions, Inc., Golden, Colorado, 1990). But be forewarned! Health risk forecasting is complicated. A truly in-depth assess-

ment of your risks would involve a longer questionnaire and an algorithmic computer program to grade
it. Many HMOs and employers offer such assessments
to their members. Find out if yours does. If you're a
company owner and want a more comprehensive test
for your employees, Johnson & Johnson Health Care
Systems, Inc. will send you a questionnaire called
Insight Health Risk Assessment. After completing the
test, you can mail it to the company for scoring and
results. Call 800-4-JNJHCS (800-456-5427) to order
or for more information. You can also find some
health risk tests on the Internet at HealthFinder
(www.healthfinder.gov).

DON'T overlook special concerns.

SUCH TESTS WILL TELL YOU if you have an extraor-
dinary health risk for which you should take extraor-
dinary investigative measures. But there are dozens of
concerns that aren't risky enough to be represented
in most questionnaires—nor prevalent enough to
merit a special mention in the sections below. Still,
something like infertility, migraine headaches, insom-
nia, acne, irritable bowels, back pain, or smoking may
worry you enormously. If you're affected by one of
them—or fear you will be—you should ask prospective HMOs these questions:

◆ **What benefits (office appointments, tests, therapy,
consultations with specialists) are available for treating this condition?**

◆ **Where does the plan draw the line in treating this
condition?** (After how many specialist consultations,
therapy appointments, etc.)

◆ **What kinds of treatments are offered for this condition?** As of 1996, Aetna Health Plan in Northern California, for example, made no particular effort to identify smokers and help them stop smoking. Harvard
Pilgrim Health Plan, on the other hand, exerts itself to
identify smokers, particularly those who are still smok-

ing despite having coronary heart disease or another dangerous condition. It also accredits local quit-smoking programs and offers members discounts to them, offers nicotine replacement systems at low prices, and has a chat room (associated with its home page on the Internet) for members who are trying to quit.

◆ **Are alternative therapies, such as biofeedback and acupuncture, covered for this condition?** Oxford Health Plans, which runs plans in New York, Connecticut, Pennsylvania, New Hampshire, and Florida, allows some members to consult acupuncturists, chiropractors, and—in Connecticut where they're licensed—naturopaths. All members can get a special rate when they are treated by acupuncturists, chiropractors, naturopaths (in Connecticut), massage therapists, yoga instructors, dietitians, and nutritionists in Oxford's network.

DO get a sneak preview of a plan.

A BILLBOARD NEAR THE Dallas airport features Barry Switzer, the coach of the Dallas Cowboys, looking over a stadium. "He picks the winners in football," the caption announces. "Now he's picked the winner in health care." NYLCare, the advertisement's sponsor, isn't the only HMO using sports celebrities to sell health care. HMOs are deploying all manner of marketing devices to make themselves attractive. The key lesson: recognize how different an HMO's selling pitch may be from reality. What you see when it's open enrollment time at your company is actually marketing literature. An HMO's brochures may describe extensive-sounding benefits and extol the plan's various features. But what such guides rarely do is explain what you won't be entitled to. And that information may prove the telling distinction that helps you choose one plan over another.

I recommend getting a foretaste of a plan by doing three things before you join. First, request a copy of the HMO's new member booklet and list of doctors and specialists. The booklet should give you the excruciating details of a plan's coverage. Look specifically at which services and conditions are excluded to understand how you could be affected. Next, call doctors to find out if they're accepting new patients from this health plan. You may have already asked the plan what percentage of its doctors have open panels to get a bead on doctor satisfaction. But this field research serves a slightly different purpose. It allows you to spot-check the statistic that an HMO gives you and, more importantly, discover if the particular doctors and specialists you want will welcome you as a member of this HMO. It wouldn't hurt to also ask the nurse-administrators how they would compare one HMO to another.

A last preview step: call customer service and fire away with questions. Ask about coverage of conditions, how their doctors are paid, how the plan scores on HEDIS measures—as much as you can think of. You aren't likely to get as many good answers as you deserve, but at least you'll get a taste of what being in this HMO is like.

HEALTH RISK ASSESSMENT TEST

EXERCISE

Endurance: How many minutes of aerobic exercise do you get each week?

	SCORE
Fewer than 15	0
15–29	3
30–44	7
45–74	10
75–119	13
120–179	17
180 or more	20

YOUR SCORE _____

Strength: How many minutes of strengthening exercise do you get each week?

	SCORE
Fewer than 15	0
15–29	1
30–44	2
45–74	3
75–119	4

YOUR SCORE _____

Flexibility: How many minutes of stretching exercise do you get each week?

	SCORE
Fewer than 15	0
15–29	1
30–44	2
45–74	3
75–119	4

YOUR SCORE _____

Light Physical Activity: How many minutes of light physical activity (such as gardening, walking, housecleaning, or golf) do you get each week?

	SCORE
Fewer than 60	0
60–119 (1–2 hours)	1
120–179 (2–3 hours)	3
180–239 (3–4 hours)	4
240–299 (4–5 hours)	5
300 or more (5 or more hours)	6

YOUR SCORE _____

YOUR TOTAL EXERCISE SCORE _____

BODY FAT

To estimate how much of your weight is body fat, refer to the table below and score yourself as follows:

Estimating Body Fat: Using the table, women should measure their hips at their widest point. Use a straight edge to connect your hip measurement with your height, and then read your percentage of body fat on the middle scale. For example, if you are 5 feet 2 inches tall and have 38-inch hips, your body is approximately 29 percent fat.

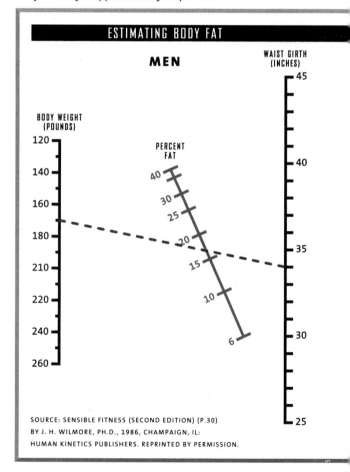

ESTIMATING BODY FAT

MEN

WAIST GIRTH
(INCHES)

BODY WEIGHT
(POUNDS)

PERCENT
FAT

SOURCE: SENSIBLE FITNESS (SECOND EDITION) (P.30)
BY J. H. WILMORE, PH.D., 1986, CHAMPAIGN, IL:
HUMAN KINETICS PUBLISHERS. REPRINTED BY PERMISSION.

MEN	WOMEN	SCORE
More than 25%	More than 30%	0
21%–25%	26–30%	3
16%–20%	21–25%	8
11%–15%	16–20%	13
10% and below	15% and below	15

YOUR TOTAL BODY FAT SCORE _____

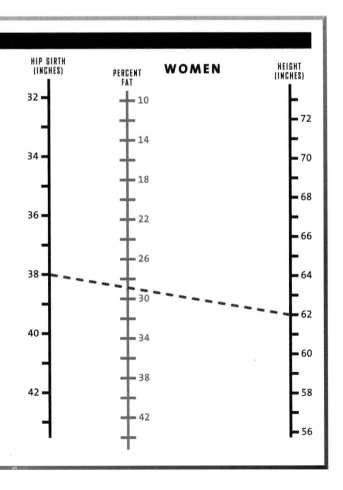

NUTRITION

Saturated Fat: How often do you eat foods high in saturated fat or cholesterol, such as butter, cream, fatty meats, hot dogs, sausages, high-fat dairy products, candy, pastries, and eggs?

	SCORE
Often (several times a day)	0
Sometimes (once every day or so)	5
Seldom (once or twice a week)	10

YOUR SCORE _____

Fiber: How often do you eat foods high in fiber, such as bran cereals, bran muffins, beans, vegetables, and fruits?

	SCORE
Often (several times a day)	6
Sometimes (once every day or so)	3
Seldom (once or twice a week)	0

YOUR SCORE _____

Sodium: How often do you eat foods high in sodium (salt), such as canned soups, hot dogs, pizza, chips, luncheon meats, pickles, and TV dinners?

	SCORE
Often (several times a day)	0
Sometimes (once every day or so)	1
Seldom (once or twice a week)	2

YOUR SCORE _____

Beta Carotene and Other Antioxidants: How often do you eat foods high in beta carotene and other antioxidants (vitamins C, E, polyphenols, lycopene)? These include yellow and dark green vegetables, such as carrots, squash, and spinach.

	SCORE
Often (several times a day)	2
Sometimes (once every day or so)	1
Seldom (once or twice a week)	0

YOUR SCORE _____

YOUR TOTAL NUTRITION SCORE _____

SMOKING

Cigarettes: How many cigarettes or cigars do you smoke
each day?

	SCORE
0	18
1–9	10
10–19	8
20–29	6
30–39	4
40–49	2
50 or more	0

YOUR SCORE _____

Pipes:

	SCORE
If you smoke only a pipe	0
Otherwise	3

YOUR SCORE _____

Smoking and the Pill (for women only):

	SCORE
If you smoke and take birth control pills	0
Otherwise	6

YOUR SCORE _____

YOUR TOTAL SMOKING SCORE _____

ALCOHOL

How many drinks do you have each day, on average?

	SCORE
0	24
1	25
2–3	12
4–5	6
6–7	3
8 or more	0

YOUR TOTAL ALCOHOL SCORE _____

ACCIDENTS

Alcohol: How many times in the last month did you drink and drive or ride with a driver who may have had too much to drink?

	SCORE
0	10
1	1
More than 1	0

YOUR SCORE _____

Mileage (automobile): In the next 12 months, how many thousands of miles will you travel by car, truck, or van?

	SCORE
Fewer than 2,000	8
2,000–5,999	6
6,000–9,999	4
10,000–19,999	1
20,000 or more	0

YOUR SCORE _____

Mileage (motorcycle): In the next 12 months, how many miles will you travel by motorcycle?

	SCORE
None	12
Fewer than 2,000	8
2,000–5,999	2
6,000–9,999	1
10,000 or more	0

YOUR SCORE _____

Safety Belts: What percentage of the time do you buckle your safety belt when driving or riding in a car?

	SCORE
0%–24%	0
25%–49%	2
50%–74%	4
75% or more	6

YOUR SCORE _____

Speed: On average, how close to the speed limit do you usually drive?

	SCORE
Within 5 mph of the speed limit	4
6–10 mph over the limit	3
11–15 mph over the limit	1
More than 15 mph over the limit	0

YOUR SCORE _____

YOUR TOTAL ACCIDENT SCORE _____

MIND-BODY INTERACTION

Just about everyone agrees that the interaction between mind and body is very important to your health, but no one has developed a satisfactory way to measure this relationship. Three measures of stress are used here. The first, the Holmes scale, measures your exposure to stressful events.

Of the three this score is most directly associated with the risk of disease.

Change. The Holmes scale lists 43 life events that have been shown to cause stress that can lead to disease. Each has been given a score. Add up the scores for all listed events that have happened to you in the last year or that you expect will occur in the near future.

THE HOLMES SCALE

1. Death of a spouse	100
2. Divorce	73
3. Marital separation	65
4. Jail term	63
5. Death of a close family member	63
6. Personal injury or illness	53
7. Marriage	50
8. Fired at work	47
9. Marital reconciliation	45
10. Retirement	45
11. Change in health of family member	44
12. Pregnancy	40
13. Sex difficulties	39
14. Gain of new family member	39
15. Business readjustment	39
16. Change in financial state	38
17. Death of a close friend	37
18. Change to different line of work	36
19. Change in number of arguments with spouse	35
20. Large mortgage	31
21. Foreclosure of mortgage or loan	30
22. Change in responsibilities at work	29
23. Son or daughter leaving home	29
24. Trouble with in-laws	29
25. Outstanding personal achievement	28
26. Spouse begins or stops work	26
27. Begin or end school	25
28. Change in living conditions	25
29. Change in personal habits	24

30. Trouble with boss	23
31. Change in work hours or conditions	20
32. Change in residence	20
33. Change in schools	20
34. Change in recreation	19
35. Change in church activities	19
36. Change in social activities	18
37. Small mortgage or loan	17
38. Change in sleeping habits	16
39. Change in number of family get-togethers	15
40. Change in eating habits	13
41. Vacation	13
42. Christmas	12
43. Minor violations of the law	11

If your total Holmes score is:

	SCORE
150 or less	6
151–250	3
251–300	1
More than 300	0

YOUR SCORE _____

Satisfaction

Life: In general, how satisfied are you with your life?

	SCORE
Very satisfied	4
Satisfied	2
Not satisfied	0

YOUR SCORE _____

Work: In general, how satisfied are you with your work?

	SCORE
Very satisfied	3
Satisfied	2
Not Satisfied	0

YOUR SCORE _____

How often do you have a really good laugh and enjoy yourself?

	SCORE
Often	2
Sometimes	1
Rarely/Never	0

YOUR SCORE _____

Coping

How often do you try to change or eliminate the causes of stressful situations?

	SCORE
Often	2
Sometimes	1
Rarely/Never	0

YOUR SCORE _____

How often do you try to change your perception of stressful situations?

	SCORE
Often	2
Sometimes	1
Rarely/Never	0

YOUR SCORE _____

How often do you practice relaxation techniques, such as meditation, progressive muscle relaxation, or the quieting reflex?

	SCORE
Often	2
Sometimes	1
Rarely/Never	0

YOUR SCORE _____

How often do you use some form of physical activity or exercise to handle stress?

	SCORE
Often	2
Sometimes	1
Rarely/Never	0

YOUR SCORE _____

How often do you talk over the stressful situations with others?

	SCORE
Often	2
Sometimes	1
Rarely/Never	0

YOUR SCORE _____

In general, how are strong are your ties with family and friends?

	SCORE
Very strong	2
About average	1
Weaker than average	0

YOUR SCORE _____

Rating Your Own Health

Considering your age, how would you describe your overall physical health?

	SCORE
Excellent	6
Good	4
Fair	2
Poor	0

YOUR SCORE _____

YOUR TOTAL MIND-BODY SCORE _____

CHOLESTEROL AND BLOOD PRESSURE

Cholesterol: If you know only your total cholesterol, use Table A. If you know your total cholesterol and your high-density lipoprotein cholesterol (HDL-C), calculate your total cholesterol/HDL-C ratio and use Table B.

TABLE A: Total Cholesterol

	SCORE
Less than 180	18
180–200	16
201–225	10
226–250	4
Over 250	0

TABLE B: Total Cholesterol: HDL-C Ratio

	SCORE
Less than 2.5	18
2.5–3.5	16
3.6–4.5	10
4.6–5.5	4
More than 5.5	0

If you do not know your cholesterol measurement, score 10.

YOUR CHOLESTEROL SCORE _____

Systolic Blood Pressure:

	SCORE
190 and above	0
160–189	1
140–159	3
120–139	6
Below 120	8

If you do not know your systolic blood pressure, score 4.

YOUR SCORE _____

Diastolic Blood Pressure:

	SCORE
115 and above	0
105–114	1
90–104	3
80–89	6
Below 80	8

If you do not know your diastolic blood pressure, score 4.

YOUR SCORE _____

YOUR TOTAL CHOLESTEROL AND BLOOD PRESSURE SCORE _____

FAMILY HEALTH

Heart Disease: How many of your immediate family members (parents, brothers or sisters) experienced a heart attack, angina (heart pain), congestive heart failure (fluid build-up in the lungs and/or legs), or stroke before the age of 50?

	SCORE
None	6
One	3
Two or more	0

YOUR SCORE _____

Diabetes: How many of your immediate family members developed diabetes before the age of 50?

	SCORE
None	4
One	2
Two or more	0

YOUR SCORE _____

Breast Cancer (for women only):

How many of your immediate family members have had breast cancer?

	SCORE
None	4
One	2
Two or more	0

YOUR SCORE _____

YOUR TOTAL FAMILY HEALTH SCORE _____

MEDICAL SCREENING TESTS

Reward yourself according to the following schedule:

	SCORE
Blood pressure check every year	0
Cholesterol testing every 3–5 years	3

For women only:

	SCORE
Mammography and physician's examination of breasts every 1–5 years after age 50	4
Pap smear every 1–3 years after age 21 or whenever regular sexual activity begins	4

YOUR SCORE _____

YOUR TOTAL SCREENING SCORE _____

FINDING YOUR LIFE SCORE

Transfer the scores from each section to the columns below:

Exercise	_____
Body Fat	_____
Nutrition	_____
Smoking	_____
Alcohol	_____
Accidents	_____
Mind-Body Interaction	_____
Cholesterol and Blood Pressure	_____
Family Health	_____
Medical Screening Tests	_____

TOTAL POINTS _____

SCORING			
		ESTIMATED LIFE EXPECTANCY	
YOUR HEALTH	LIFESCORE	MEN	WOMEN
Excellent	Above 200	81 or more	85 or more
Good	176–200	78–80	82–84
Average	151–175	73–77	77–81
Below average	125–150	70–72	72–76
Poor	Less than 125	69 or less	71 or less

"Health Risk Assessment Test" from LifePlan: Your Own Master Plan for Maintaining Health and Preventing Illness, *by Donald M. Vickery, M.D. (Health Decisions, Inc., Golden, Colorado, 1990).*

YOUNG AND GROWING FAMILIES

YOU'RE YOUNG, YOU'RE HEALTHY, but you're still a huge consumer of health care services. Why? Simple. Getting pregnant and having babies requires a lot of medical attention. A look at the tables following this profile of the most common procedures and services tells the story. The care required before a baby is born, during delivery, and after birth so dominate a young family's medical needs that childbirth measures should be a key way you judge health plans. Between ear infections, sore throats, vaccinations, and monthly well-baby visits, kids are big health care consumers, too. But here it's the quantity of health care used that's so striking. So, in addition to thinking about the quality of a plan's kid care, you should look carefully at how easily and quickly you'll be able to get that care. Here's how a family of two young adults (between the ages of 24 and 40) with young children, or with plans to have children, can find the best HMO:

DO recognize the significance of prenatal care.

NO ONE NEEDS TO TELL YOU that a huge array of potential problems in childbirth—and with the baby itself—can be averted with attentive care during pregnancy. The questions is, how well does an HMO act on this knowledge? The best HMOs cover and test as many members as they can during their first three months of pregnancy. If they do that well, they're far more likely to be sharper at spotting and solving problems early, which is exactly what you want. The top scorers in the country—with 100 percent prenatal screening—were NorthMed in Traverse City, Michigan, Providence Health Plan of Oregon, and Cigna of Colorado, according to Quality Compass, a database assembled by the National Committee for Quality Assurance in Washington, D.C. Look for a "prenatal care during the first trimester" rate that's better than the national average of 87.5 percent.

DON'T accept needless surgery.

SURGERY INVITES COMPLICATIONS, even with routine procedures such as Caesarean sections. There are two signs that an HMO is philosophically committed to avoiding needless surgery. First, it will have a C-section rate of below 15 percent, much lower than the national average of 19.93 percent. Among the lowest in the country, according to Quality Compass: Cigna of San Diego, at 3.3 percent; Prudential of Colorado, at 9.2 percent; and Prudential of Northern California, at 9.3 percent.

The second sign, as described in Chapter 2, is that the plan will be able to tell you its VBAC rate, or the percentage of women who deliver vaginally after having previously had a C-section. At this point, the VBAC rate itself isn't as significant as the fact that an HMO is able to report one. It's an extremely positive signal that the plan has shed an outdated obstetrics concept that could be dangerous to you.

DO insist upon satisfied obstetricians, gynecologists, and pediatricians.

AT THIS STAGE, YOUR FAMILY will depend upon this trio of doctors far more often than a primary care doctor. You want to find a plan that allows you to easily find an OB/Gyn or pediatrician—and readily switch to a new one, if you need to. You'll also want a plan that's doing a good job of keeping these specialists reasonably happy. The answer: look for OB/Gyns and pediatricians with "open panels," which simply means they're accepting new patients from a particular plan. HMOs with the highest percentage of open-panel OB/Gyns and pediatricians will probably be far more available to you. A high percentage of open panels also means that doctors are satisfied with the HMO's policies and compensation—or they'd find a way to bar new patients. The rate you should look for: 90 percent or higher.

DO demand high childhood immunization rates.

VACCINATIONS ARE ONE of the cheapest and easiest ways to keep kids healthy and disease free, so if an HMO scores below the national average of 77.7 percent, beware. You should seek out much higher rates. The country's top-scoring plans in this area are Central Minnesota Group Health Plan in St. Cloud, Minnesota; Welborn Health Plans of Evansville, Indiana; and Columbia Medical Plan in Columbia, Maryland; with rates of 96 percent to 99.4 percent.

DON'T neglect the classic kids' condition.

YOU MAY NEVER HAVE STRUGGLED for breath in your life, but asthma could still be a problem for your kids. The number of kids (and adults) with asthma has been gradually increasing since the early 1900s. About 8 percent of kids have some kind of asthma, causing an estimated 10 million missed days of school and 200,000 hospitalizations a year. But even if your kids don't develop it, an HMO's response to asthma is an excellent barometer of its approach to childhood conditions. Why? Asthma challenges a health plan's competence on several levels. Because the condition can be aggravated by such a broad range of irritants and activities, finding the most effective medicine is tricky. Preventing emergency hospitalizations and missed days of school also depends upon how well doctors teach parents and children to manage their condition.

Many health plans can tell you the percentage of asthmatic kids who are admitted to the hospital each year, but unfortunately, the measure isn't a really good indicator. Instead, ask an HMO what it's doing to reduce the number of admissions due to asthma.

The plan should be able to describe a specific and comprehensive program. Harvard Community Health Plan, for example, has an excellent asthma-management program which includes readily available peak flow meters, a device to aid breathing; easy access to specialists; and visits to members' homes, so that HMO doctors can assess a member's home environment. The key characteristics of a good asthma program include:

◆**Doctors who specialize in asthma.** If the HMO asks primary care doctors to handle asthma, the plan should have a well-established referral path to gather more information from allergists or pulmonologists, for example.

◆**Leading-edge medication.** HMOs often define which drugs doctors must use. Such "restricted formularies frequently lag behind in providing the best drugs available, especially in asthma care," says Dr. Richard Weber, a staff physician at the National Jewish Research and Medical Center in Denver, Colorado. In 1997 two of the best asthma medications were Serevent, a long-lasting bronchodialator, and Flowvent (fluticasone is the generic name), a potent steroid inhalant. If those drugs aren't on the list of an HMO's allowable medications—and Proventil, a less-convenient bronchodialator (generically known as albuterol) is—then the plan isn't determined to offer the very best in asthmatic care.

◆**Quality-of-life asthma measures.** Truly excellent plans are measuring their performance not only with hard-core outcomes, such as the percentage of asthmatics who were hospitalized, but with softer gauges that assess how well—or sick—members feel. If you find a plan that can report on how many missed days of work and school its asthmatics had, how often they felt unwell, and how much medication they've used, you've discovered a top-notch HMO.

DO find out who subs for your pediatrician.

MOST OF US THINK OF OUR children's health care as falling into two categories: routine and emergency. But there is actually a third: urgent, when your child needs to be seen today, but not necessarily within the next hour. You should have a clear picture of who will be fielding your call and what kind of response you can expect in each of these three situations. Will another pediatrician always be covering when yours is unavailable? Or will your after-hours call be handled by a pediatric nurse or a trained operator? Will the HMO try to diagnose and advise you over the phone, or will you be certain to get an in-person consultation? Where will you have to travel for routine, urgent, and emergency child care?

DON'T be too easy to please.

INTENSIVE USE OF HEALTH CARE services means intensive interaction with an HMO. If you have a question about how your plan works, what's covered, or any other detail, the last thing you want is to hear endless ringing after you dial the plan's customer service number. HMOs often publish all kinds of measures describing how fast their customer service and claims departments pick up the phone, but unfortunately they're not usually comparable. The only one that's fairly reliable: what percentage of calls into customer service go unanswered and are "abandoned"? An HMO that has an abandoned-call rate of under 3 percent is doing a top-notch job. This isn't a HEDIS yardstick, but most HMOs track such information for their internal use and for corporate customers.

DO plan on the unexpected.

NO ONE PLANS UPON NEEDING psychological counseling. But here's a reality check: nearly half of all adults will consult with a mental health practitioner in their lifetime, according to the American Psycho-

logical Association. Psychological evaluations and
therapy are certainly one of the most commonly
used services at all ages. There were more than 25
million such appointments in 1994, the majority for
adults between the ages of 25 and 64. "The thirties
and forties are high-stress periods. You've got families with two jobs, kids, midlife issues. All of the sud-
den you throw in a job crisis, and a couple can fall
apart," says Sue Sheffler, president of Sheffler &
Associates, a health care consulting group in Arlington, Massachusetts.

Obviously, the smart thing is to at least evaluate a
health plan's coverage and quality in these areas. If
you never need them, terrific. If you do require intervention, however, a good mental health or substance
abuse program is truly critical, but by no means
assured. Employers and HMOs have savagely cut benefits and coverage to reduce costs. Employers spent
about $100 per employee for mental health services
in 1996, down from about $400 a decade ago. "Men-
tal health services are one of the easiest areas to cut
out because there is no resistance," says health care
consultant Dwight McNeill. A sense of vulnerability
and a lingering stigma associated with needing psychological intervention make depressed and troubled
people uniquely ill-equipped to battle such cuts by
HMOs and other insurers.

The first barometer of an HMO's diligence in
addressing mental health problems is the one
described in Chapter 2: What percentage of members
who've been hospitalized with a mental disorder
received a follow-up phone call or had a follow-up
appointment within 30 days of their discharge? You
have to be really sick to be admitted for a mental disorder these days. Not to track patients after they're
discharged is disgraceful. The best HMOs follow up
on 96 percent of such patients, according to Sheffler
& Associates. The national average for the 300 HMOs

that the firm tracks? Just 74.8 percent.

Next look for the following attributes of effective mental health programs:

◆ **Self-referral.** You shouldn't have to embarrass yourself by asking your primary care doctor to okay a consultation with a psychologist.

◆ **In-person diagnosis.** If your concerns are worrisome enough to drive you to consult a psychologist, they're personal enough to be heard face-to-face by a psychologist. Over-the-phone diagnoses aren't as thorough.

◆ **Unlimited benefits for people with severe psychiatric disorders** (such as schizophrenia or a manic depressive disorder). An HMO will limit the number of sessions available for less extreme problems, but the best programs give you 10 to 20 sessions before reevaluating your case. Warning: there's increasingly a big discrepancy between what a plan says it will offer you and what you're most likely to get. "Many say you have up to 20 or 30 sessions a year. However, if therapists in the network average more than five or six sessions, they get kicked out," says Karen Shore, a psychologist and president of the National Coalition of Mental Health Professionals and Consumers, in Commack, New York. Call therapists in the managed care network to find out what their experience has been.

TOP FIVE OUTPATIENT SERVICES FOR KIDS

SERVICE	NUMBER OF OCCURRENCES
Throat culture and other microscopic examinations	6.8 million
Miscellaneous manual examinations and measurements	4.0 million
Pap smear test and cell block	3.5 million
Eye examination	3.0 million
Gynecologic examination	2.3 million

SOURCE, PGS. 82–84: HCIA INC., BALTIMORE, MD

MOST COMMON HOSPITAL PROCEDURES

For Boys (0–13 years)

PROCEDURE	NUMBER OF OCCURRENCES
Circumcision	852,965
Spinal tap	69,068
Vaccination	68,540
Appendectomy	26,360
Phototherapy (for jaundiced newborns)	25,071

MOST COMMON HOSPITAL PROCEDURES

For Girls (0–13 years)

PROCEDURE	NUMBER OF OCCURRENCES
Vaccination	170,043
Spinal tap	55,820
Phototherapy (for jaundiced newborns)	24,272
Appendectomy	21,643
Insert endotrachea tube	19,331

TOP FIVE OUTPATIENT SERVICES

For Adults (25–44 years)

SERVICE	NUMBER OF OCCURRENCES
Pap smear test and cell block	11.1 million
Psychotherapy	6.0 million
Miscellaneous manual examinations and measurements	5.7 million
Gynecologic examination	5.4 million
Eye exam	2.5 million

MOST COMMON HOSPITAL PROCEDURES

For Women (18–39 years)

PROCEDURE	NUMBER OF OCCURRENCES
Assistance delivering a baby	681,445
Caesarean section	523,781
Episiotomy	462,395
Repair tears resulting from delivery	366,080
Delivery via vacuum (with episiotomy)	136,259

MOST COMMON HOSPITAL PROCEDURES

For Men (18–39 years)

PROCEDURE	NUMBER OF OCCURRENCES
Removal of appendix	51,696
Back surgery (disc removal)	49,218
Alcohol detoxification	40,562
Repair fractured leg	24,106
Removal of lesion or skin tissue	23,394

PROFILE 2

MIDDLE-AGED PARENTS
WITH TEENAGERS

THESE ARE TRICKY YEARS. If you've been healthy through your twenties and thirties, all you've needed is infrequent and very routine health care. If your genes blessed you and you've sidestepped major health eroders like smoking, excess weight, and alcohol abuse, that's all you may require for years to come. But if cholesterol and calories flock to you, you're vulnerable. When back pain or heart disease—two very common conditions in this age group—make an unwelcome entrance into your life, the medical attention you receive should be far from routine. Poor quality could mean years of pain, or even premature death.

By now your kids have outgrown the stream of immunizations, fevers, and infections of their younger years. For them, also, the health issues that can arise are far more consequential. Adolescents and teenagers may need counseling, drug and/or alcohol intervention, or abortion services. No parent wants to admit that their children will ever need any of these services, but they often do. My advice: Equip yourself for these needs by picking the right plan, so that you'll be in great shape whether your children ever use the services or not. Here's how two middle-aged parents (between the ages of 40 and 64), with teen-aged children, should find the best plan:

DO shop for early heart care.

YOU'RE TREADING PRIME heart disease territory now. Nearly a million Americans die each year from coronary-artery disease—half of them from heart attacks. Another 800,000 undergo heart bypass or angioplasty surgery every year. At their best, managed care companies flag members at risk of heart disease and intervene early to change their eating and exercise habits. At worst, they ignore the problem until a heart attack sends a patient through the doors flat on his back. The most basic measure of a plan's attentiveness here is its cholesterol screening rate. The top scorers in the country, such as PCA Healthplan of Florida (South), Welborn Healthplan (in Evansville, Indiana), and Fallon Community Health Plan (in Worcester, Massachusetts), measure cholesterol levels in 88 percent or more of their eligible members, compared to just 68.5 percent nationally.

Another sign of excellent early cardiac care is a well-coordinated system for changing the habits of members with a high risk of heart disease. Look for a program that offers one-to-one as well as classroom education, exercise incentives, and close monitoring of members' progress.

Finally, examine a HMO's drug program for preventing first and second heart attacks. One litmus test: What is the plan's policy on "statins," a new class of powerful but expensive cholesterol-lowering drugs? (Bristol-Myers Squibb's product is known as Pravachol.) Clinical trials have shown that anyone who has had a heart attack or bypass surgery should be on statins, yet only about 25 percent of such folks are taking the drug. Forward-thinking HMOs such as Group Health Cooperative of Puget Sound have decided that the cost of statins isn't as high as heart surgery expenses would be without the pills. So in 1996 it tripled its budget for statins, to $3 million a year. Even members who haven't yet had a heart attack, but have heart disease or a high risk of developing it, have access to the drug.

DON'T settle for poor cardiac results.

IF IT DOES ITS JOB WELL, an HMO should be able to lower the number of times it has to actually cut open patients to save their hearts. Judge a plan's results by looking at its angioplasty and heart bypass rates together, as described in Chapter 2. Independent Health in Buffalo, New York, for example, has a low angioplasty rate of 2.63 procedures per thousand men between the ages of 45 and 64. That's not necessarily a sign of early and successful intervention, though, because its bypass rate, as reported by Quality Compass in 1996, was 11.33, nearly three times as high as the national average.

The best practice rate identified by Sheffler & Associates is 1.6 angioplasties and 1.5 bypasses per thousand men between the ages of 45 and 64. While no plans in Quality Compass's database met both of those performance measures, CFS HealthGroup (in Baltimore, Maryland) and Cigna Florida (South Florida) scored very well on both procedure rates. In contrast, PCA Health Plan of Florida (North) and Independent Health's Buffalo and Hudson/Metro groups sported the highest bypass rates, ranging from 9.8 to 11.9 per thousand. Angioplasties at NYLCare Gulfcoast (in Texas), Healthsource (Indiana), and Health Network (Colorado Springs, Colorado) were among the highest posted on Quality Compass, ranging from 11.33 to 19.23 per thousand. If your HMO candidates don't meet Sheffler's high standard, compare their rates to the national averages: 4.8 per 1,000 for angioplasties and 4.1 per 1,000 for bypasses.

DO study a plan's breast cancer outcomes.

A BROAD SIGNAL OF A PLAN'S seriousness in tackling breast cancer, one of the few cancers that is becoming more common, is a high mammography rate. Sheffler & Associates says an 85 percent rate among women between 52 and 64 (who've had a screening within the last two years) is exemplary. The national average is only 68.5 percent.

But middle-aged women need to probe beyond this simple prevention statistic. A true measure of a plan's success is how many breast cancer patients it saves. Ask a plan for its five-year survival rate for "Stage II" breast cancer. Only about 10 percent of all HMOs will be able to give you this rate, so it's a good sign if they can. Ideally, you'll be able to compare one HMO's rate to another's to judge how well they're battling this cancer. Alternatively, you may be able to evaluate how the rate has changed over the last two or three years.

A plan that's serious about lowering the incidence of breast cancer, such as Kaiser Permanente Northwest and Group Health Cooperative of Puget Sound, is adopting FACCT breast cancer gauges, or something similar. If so, it will be able to tell you, in hard numbers:

◆ How many breast cancers were detected early rather than later.

◆ How many women with Stage I or Stage II breast cancer undergo breast conserving surgery (usually a lumpectomy) rather than mastectomy and receive radiation therapy after surgery.

◆ How satisfied women were with the information they received before making their surgery decision and with their access to specialists and other services.

◆ How well women felt they coped with the cancer, the treatment, and their routine life activities.

DON'T forget the other cancer threat.

CERVICAL CANCER SCREENING (a Pap test) should be even more well-entrenched than mammography at health plans. The best practice rate, according to Sheffler & Associates, is 84.9 percent. The national average of 300 HMOs was only 73.2 percent. Because the error rate on Pap tests is high, look for an HMO that readily offers a thin prep vaginal smear test, which is more expensive but produces much more reliable results.

DO not accept high hysterectomy rates.

HYSTERECTOMIES ARE BY far the most common reason women in this age group are hospitalized in this country. What's awful is that many hysterectomies shouldn't be taking place at all. There are a number of less invasive alternatives for solving fibroids and other uterine problems to yanking out a woman's uterus. Unfortunately, that up-to-date knowledge hasn't filtered through to many doctors and plans. The great disparity between hysterectomy rates in different parts of the country and among different health plans tells you how important it is to check an HMO's score in this area.

A low rate signifies a bias against surgery, which is good, as well as a modern understanding of women's health issues. Sheffler & Associates' best practice rate is 4.3 hysterectomies per 1,000 members between the ages of 45 and 64, while the national average is 9.14 per thousand. Best performers according to Quality Compass are Health New England, with a 4.24 rate, Kaiser Permanente-Hawaii, at 4.65, and HealthAmerica, in Pittsburgh, at 4.76. Who's performing too many hysterectomies? Health Network in Colorado Springs, Colorado, PCA Health Plan of Florida (North), and Prudential of Kansas City, Kansas, reported hysterectomies ranging from 19.9 percent to 31.23 percent.

DON'T overlook addiction problems.

ALCOHOL AND DRUG ADDICTION is so common that detoxification is one of the top five reasons why boys and men are hospitalized from ages 14 to 64. That statistic is all the more stunning when you know that people are sent to hospitals to get sober far less frequently than they used to be. You can tell how seriously a health plan tackles addiction problems in a number of ways. If the plans "carves out" the care, by subcontracting with a managed behavioral health company, it's obviously less involved in setting standards for the care, giving the care, and coordinating it with the rest of a members' health services than a plan that takes on the job itself. A second attribute to look for: a program with a long history. Kaiser Permanente in Oakland, California, for example, has a highly regarded chemical dependency recovery program that's more than two decades old. Here are some key features that make it successful:

◆ **Ease of entry.** About half of the members who enter Kaiser's program refer themselves—no questions asked. Family members and Kaiser doctors frequently recommend members join the program.

◆ **Varying intensity.** The treatment level depends upon a member's addiction level. But no matter where a member enters the program, their involvement will taper off gradually rather than abruptly. Only the most dependent members begin treatment with hospitalization. "Patients who just can't stop using are put into the hospital for three to five days," says Robert Boyd, program director. Most addicted members begin with "day treatment," which consists of eight-hour sessions at Kaiser's center for two weeks. That's followed by two to three months of shorter sessions (two to three hours) six times each week. Next is six months of visiting the center three times a week. And finally, a recovering member returns to the center once a week for another two years. Random drug and alcohol tests are administered throughout the program.

◆ **Uses multiple disciplines.** The goal of the program is abstinence, and a crucial way to achieve it is to help members learn how to cope with normal life. "Because many people have been medicating themselves with drugs or alcohol, they never learn how to deal with joy, depression—the full range of normal social feelings," explains Boyd. Another route to success is to catch and properly treat members with a co-existing mental disorder—about a third of patients who are in the program. To accomplish these tasks, Kaiser relies on professionals with a broad range of credentials. They include psychiatrists, nurse practitioners, psychologists, social workers, and family and marriage counselors. The intake worker, who interviews members entering the program, is a certified alcohol and drug counselor.

◆ **Linked to community.** To be successful, recovering members need to forge new social ties. Kaiser's recovery agenda requires its patients to join a self-help program (such as Alcoholics Anonymous) that meets at least twice a week and stay in it for the duration of the program.

◆ **Long-term scope.** Someone who enters Kaiser's program at the beginning is likely to be involved in it for more than three years. That's a very large committment of time and resources for a health plan—perhaps the best single sign of the program's excellence.

DO analyze an HMO's approach to depression.

DEPRESSION IS ASTONISHINGLY common. It may manifest itself once, for just a short period, in a lifetime. Or it may be a lifelong periodic affliction. Some 15 percent of all adults are suffering from depression at any given time. An MIT study estimated that in 1990, depression and mood disorders cost $43.7 billion. It's worth investigating a plan's approach to depression because it's the most obvious place to start improving mental health services—and it's more likely to befall you than any of the other affective disorders. But judging a plan's abilities is especially tricky because they often unload the whole job of treating members onto a mental health vendor. Also, measuring degrees of wellness in mental health is as murky as pea soup to the health establishment—so they haven't tried very hard to do it.

As a backdrop to your investigation of a plan's abilities, understand that most people in this country get attention for mental and emotional problems from someone other than a specialist. That pattern plays right into HMOs' preference for primary care physicians to handle most member problems. Unfortunately, it also leads to really poor solutions for many of us. "When primary care physicians treat, they frequently do not use a high enough dose, so they may not be administering drugs at therapeutic levels. And many times the physician is not even identifying that a person is depressed," explains Donald Steinwachs, a professor and department head at Johns Hopkins University in Baltimore, Maryland. "Underdiagnosis and undertreatment is a major problem with depression."

The first question to ask: How good are the HMOs' primary care physicians at spotting depression? Chances are that HMOs with doctors on staff will be much better than HMOs with large group practices or doctor networks. Why? They have a much easier time schooling their docs on the traits of this subtle condition or mandating that doctors incorporate a brief screening questionnaire into members' routine checkups, for example. In addition to the program attributes noted above (in the Young Family Profile), an HMO which excels in diagnosing and treating depression will:

◆ **Judge your need with pros.** If your primary care doctor refers you, the health plan arranges a face-to-face interview with someone who decides whether you'll go to a social worker or a psychologist. Plans that use a Ph.D. or clinician with a master's degree to make that judgment are best for you. An interview with someone who has a bachelor degree (but who has access to a Ph.D. on site as a backup) is next best.

◆ **Have an intake protocol.** The mental health portion of your plan should have a clear process your provider follows when it brings a patient in. Is there a flow chart that shows each step the plan takes to assure proper assessment of your condition, coordination with your primary care doctor, a timely first appointment and review?

◆ **Have an up-to-date formulary.** Some of the new antidepressants and antipsychotic drugs such as Zyprexa or Clozaril are terribly expensive. Is the HMO cheaping out by not allowing them to be prescribed?

◆ **Let you stay on drugs.** This sounds awful, but it actually isn't. According to Dr. Daniel Ford, an associate professor at Johns Hopkins, all evidence is showing that patients do better with longer-term treatment. Yet many HMOs are asking members to try to wean themselves from antidepressants after six to 12 months. "The data is now showing that if someone has had more than two or three episodes with depression, they should be on antidepressants for five years—or maybe a lifetime," says Ford.

A last way to compare health plans is to apply FACCT new depression measures. Some plans, such as Blue Cross Blue Shield of Massachusetts, don't use the FACCT measures described below, but have developed their own tools for assessing the potency of their mental health services. Look for one vital component in these gauges: members reporting on their own sense of well-being and daily functioning. That, after all, is the real measure of whether a person is getting better, and the one you are most interested in. The FACCT measures on depression, which only a handful of HMOs in the country were starting to adopt by early 1997, include:

◆ Measurement of patients' bond with their psychologists and ability to get the care they need.

◆ A gauge of patients' satisfaction with the respect and attention they're given.

◆ An assessment of patients' satisfaction with their specialists' skill and with the results of their treatment.

◆ The number of patients whose condition improves significantly within six months.

◆ How well patients are able to continue their daily work activities six months after diagnosis.

◆ How well patients cope, socially and emotionally, after treatment.

DON'T ignore the mental health carve-out issue.

BECAUSE MENTAL HEALTH eats up so much money with results that are, in the eyes of many HMOs, completely unpredictable, most HMOs have just disposed of this particular headache by giving the job to someone else. Usually it's a giant vendor, such as Value Behavioral Health, in Avon, Connecticut, or Magellan Health Services, in Atlanta, Georgia.

The positive aspects of a carve-out program are that you often don't need a referral to get into it and that it may offer members more privacy—extremely important, since most people aren't thrilled about their employer knowing that they're seeing a psychologist, social worker, or psychiatrist. But there is a serious drawback: coordination between your primary care doctor and your psychologist is dramatically diminished. Most HMOs have never met the mental health professional they're sending their patient to. "They may not have even talked to them on the phone," says Ford. "Yet the more we learn about depression the more we know that coordination with a primary care doctor is very important at the beginning of mental health treatment and at the end."

If your prospective HMOs "carves out" mental health, do yourself a favor and take the extra step of interviewing some of the psychologists in the plans. They should be able to tell you immediately how many sessions for different conditions are allowed by different plans and mental health vendors. Ask particularly about depression and counseling for adolescents, teenagers, and alcohol or drug abuse.

DO evaluate teen needs.

YOUR TEENAGER IS AT RISK for a whole range of behavioral and physical pitfalls that often go undetected. Between 30 percent and 40 percent of teenaged girls have babies. Drug and alcohol detoxification is the fourth most common reason boys between the ages of 14 and 17 were hospitalized in 1996, according to HCIA Inc., a health care information company in Baltimore.

You, of course, are your teen's first line of defense against such difficulties. But a health plan can help immensely. Find out what a plan asks its primary care physicians to assess during your child's yearly physicals. Docs who are asked to screen kids for drug use, smoking, and depression will be able to spot problems early and help you intervene. Also look for a plan that offers well-designed educational programs on sex, smoking, drugs, and alcohol. Make sure your teen can get into these programs readily and take advantage of them. Easy access to mental health benefits, including a serious chemical dependency program, is a must. In addition

TOP FIVE OUTPATIENT SERVICES

For Adults (45–64 years)

SERVICE	NUMBER OF OCCURRENCES
Pap smear test and cellblock	6.2 million
Electrocardiogram	5.1 million
Miscellaneous manual examinations and measurements	4.9 million
Eye exam	4.9 million
Removal of lesion or skin through cryosurgery, laser, or other means	3.8 million

MOST COMMON HOSPITAL PROCEDURES

For Boys (14–17 years)

PROCEDURE	NUMBER OF OCCURRENCES
Appendectomy	13,800
Chemotherapy	6,714
Repair fractured leg	4,138
Alcohol/drug rehabilitation	2,393
Spinal tap	2,189

MOST COMMON HOSPITAL PROCEDURES

For Girls (14–17 years)

PROCEDURE	NUMBER OF OCCURRENCES
Assistance delivering a baby	47,404
Episiotomy	32,745
Caesarean section	20,679
Repair tears resulting from delivery	20,267
Appendectomy	12,627

SOURCE, PGS. 95–96: HCIA INC., BALTIMORE, MD

MOST COMMON HOSPITAL PROCEDURES

For Men (40–64 years)

PROCEDURE	NUMBER OF OCCURRENCES
Angioplasty	101,373
Left heart catheterization	96,913
Back surgery (removal of disc)	63,346
Alcohol detoxification	51,132
Biopsy of esophogus, stomach, or small intestine	39,016

MOST COMMON HOSPITAL PROCEDURES

For Women (40–64 years)

PROCEDURE	NUMBER OF OCCURRENCES
Total hysterectomy	166,221
Vaginal hysterectomy	77,640
Gallbladder removal by laparoscopy	66,274
Left heart catheterization	59,665
Back surgery (disc removal)	49,553

to the key characteristics of an addiction recovery program described previously, look for an agenda that requires heavy parental involvement. "When parents are not involved in the child's recovery effort, the chances of success are much worse," says Janet Kirk, director of adolescent chemical dependency services at Kaiser Permanente in Walnut Creek, California.

CHAPTER

4

CHRONICALLY ILL AND Seniors

THE NEWS IS NOT GOOD for you. While HMOs can do a bang-up job of caring for the young and relatively healthy, they fail more frequently with the chronically sick and the elderly. Dr. John Ware at the New England Medical Center recently documented this fact in a four-year study of 2,235 patients with four chronic conditions. He found that "for elderly patients treated under Medicare, declines in physical health were more common in HMOs than in fee-for-service plans." In fact, 54 percent of HMO members studied showed declines compared to just 28 percent in traditional Medicare, where doctors are reimbursed for their services.

Those numbers are shocking for two reasons. First, an enormous number of us fall into this category. Nearly 100 million Americans have

chronic diseases or disabilities, according to researchers at Institute for Health & Aging at the University of California in San Francisco. Second, if you're burdened with a chronic condition or over 65, you're far more vulnerable than the young and healthy. It's unconscionable to be shortchanged on health care when you need it most.

Needless to say, you should treat selection of an HMO with the utmost deliberation. There are an array of special dimensions you need to analyze in addition to the characteristics described in Chapters 1 and 2. While I've separated issues for the chronically ill and people over 65 into different profiles below, seniors should take care to read both sections because recurring and complex health conditions are so much more likely to develop as you age. Even if you and your spouse are healthy now, you'll want an HMO that can see you both through the worst that could happen.

PROFILE 3

FAMILIES WITH CHRONIC CONDITIONS OR SERIOUS ILLNESSES

HEALTH CARE BECOMES AN obsession for families with chronic conditions or major illnesses. Getting it, paying for it, and benefiting from it dominates their lives—and yet it's rarely accessible, affordable, and of good quality. Managed care's great promise—that it will coordinate its resources to provide superior results—often proves completely false for such families. Janet McCarron, a community nurse in Chicago who's the mother of a daughter with a mild case of cerebral palsy, has tested health plans for 14 years. "My husband and I have been our daughter's case manager. HMOs and preferred provider organizations (PPOs) have not," she says. "We were the ones who fought for what she needed and fought to get it paid for."

More of us are chronically sick than you'd guess. Almost a quarter of all adults between 45 and 64 were limited by such a condition in 1994, and more than 40 percent of that group were unable to carry on with their jobs or housework. The basic problem for such people is that health insurance is designed to respond to emergencies. Folks with chronic conditions certainly have health crises, but they could have far fewer if more money were spent on treatment that improves daily life and prevents the need for more drastic measures later. In Ronnie McCarron's case, for example, regular physical therapy to loosen tight inner thigh muscles, year in and year out, not only allows her to walk smoothly, it prevents or reduces the need for surgical release of those muscles.

Managed care plans, which constantly tout their emphasis on prevention, should be the first to subscribe to such a health care strategy but often aren't. They also fail to accommodate other terrifically important needs of chronically ill members. Of the estimated 99 million people with persistent health problems in 1995, 41 million could not fully perform daily living activities, such as dressing and eating, according to the Robert Wood Johnson Foundation, in Princeton, New Jersey.

Families of children with cerebral palsy, myelodysplasia, cystic fibrosis, muscular dystrophy, diabetes, and other conditions face particularly painful and difficult issues. HealthPartners, a mixed model HMO in Minneapolis, along with PACER, a local parent advocacy coalition, and the Center for Children With Chronic Illness and Disability, a research and training center at the University of Minnesota, collaborated on a study of such families' needs. Many families had difficulty understanding and navigating the referral system. Nearly a third said that caretaking barred them from full-time employment. Almost 90 percent reported needing help to manage stress. HealthPartners's doctors reported that although such children made up only a tiny percentage of their patient load, they devoted 6 to 20 percent of their time to kids with special needs—yet still had insufficient time with patients to review reports, evaluate medications, and coordinate care.

In the face of such obstacles, finding an HMO that

can address your family's very particular needs is paramount. You have one key advantage over families with normal health issues: you know what your health problem is. So you already have a crystal clear picture of the areas of excellence you're looking for. Finding them may still be very difficult. But as you also already know, taking good care of a chronic condition means being more diligent about your research and more persistent about demanding attention. Here are some extra steps to help you uncover the quality you deserve:

DON'T fall for a faux HMO.

THERE'S NO SUCH THING as a fake HMO, of course. But they come in so many permutations now that it's very easy to lose sight of a central fact about managed care: most of it isn't managed at all. In other words, the fastest-growing and most common types of HMOs are not carefully monitoring, coordinating, and communicating all aspects of your care throughout the organization, as the term "managed care" implies. Most are woefully behind in using computers and software to pool information on members and make it readily accessible to medical personnel. In fact, many HMOs are really insurance companies in a new guise. They contract with doctors, specialists, hospitals, and other providers of medical care and then try to influence them to behave in a cost-conscious way, usually through financial incentives and penalties. For this reason I call them "faux" HMOs.

They could be using their networks to truly collaborate about and improve tremendously upon the care you get. The difference between a faux HMO and a company that truly manages your care may not matter much when you have routine health problems. But it can transform your life if you have a chronic condition.

My suggestion: Look for a staff or group model

HMO rather than a network or IPA (for independent practice association). A staff model HMO hires its own doctors and is far more likely to have perfected the sharing of information and multidisciplinary cooperation that is so vital to caring for a complex and ongoing condition. There's a drawback that may overwhelm the advantages of following this advice. If you have a longstanding relationship with a doctor who has done an exceptional job of treating you, you may be better off joining the plan that allows you to stick with him or her. Understand, though, that your experience with this doctor could change depending upon the plan's limitations. A terrific doctor can only do so much if her recommendations for physical therapy or home visits or specialists are thwarted by an unresponsive or overly cost-conscious HMO.

DO seek people like yourself.

A GOOD BET FOR FINDING an HMO that does a good job with your diabetes, lung disease, degenerative joint disease, or other chronic illness is to find one that has many members with the same condition. A plan is much more likely to try to systematically improve its results with a given illness if enough of its members suffer from it. Ask how many members in the plan have your condition. "If they can't tell you, that's a warning sign," counsels Teresa Fama, deputy director of Chronic Care Initiative in HMOs, a Robert Wood Johnson Foundation program.

Next, find out if the plan has a special program to treat your condition, often called a "disease management program." One of the most impressive examples: a program for HIV-infected members launched by Harvard Community Health Plan in 1986. An HIV consultation team (consisting of two part-time infectious disease specialists, two full-time hematologists/oncologists, five full-time HIV resource nurses, a program assistant, and a part-time secretary) helps primary care physicians minister to 750 members with HIV. The program, which focuses on early intervention, education, and home care services, revolves heavily around an "HIV resource" nurse. She educates members and doctors about different therapies and medications, makes home visits, helps with hospitalization and discharge, and acts as a liaison to community groups. Another vital element in the program is communication. Consultation team members meet weekly to discuss the status of HIV patients. The program has successfully reduced patient hospitalization and cut the length of stay from 8.55 days in 1991 to 5.24 days in 1995. As important, HIV patient satisfaction was much higher than that of patients who are treated in HIV clinics.

DON'T let a lousy disease management program win you over.

LET'S SAY AN HMO PASSES your first two tests: it has a lot of patients with your exact condition, and it runs a special program for them. These are great signals that your health condition may be handled with sensitivity and sophistication. But probe further. Does the disease management program use nationally recognized guidelines? Take asthma, for example. The Agency for Health Care Policy and Research (www.ahcpr.gov) has issued extensive guidelines for mild through severe cases of asthma. The book-length set of directions includes drug recommendations, patient education techniques, and emergency instructions *(right)*. In June of 1977, the AHCPR expanded its role as a guideline developer by establishing an evidence-based practice program, in which it awarded five-year contracts to 12 U.S. and Canadian institutions to study all pertinent scientific literature on a medical topic. Another publisher of well-recognized guidelines: the National Heart Lung and Blood Institute, which is part of the

National Institutes of Health. Beginning in the fall of 1998, a National Guidelines Clearinghouse on the Web will house a full range of guidance on treatments for special conditions. In the meantime you can search for guidelines via the Web's Healthfinder (www.healthfinder.gov).

Look hard at a disease management program's education component, also. The more education that you'll get from an HMO about a disease—preferably

THE RIGHT STUFF

ANY FAMILY WITH A CHRONIC condition or illness should equip itself with the best information available about it. You should particularly distinguish between a sketchy disease management program at an HMO and one that adheres to nationally recognized guidelines. The Agency for Health Care Policy and Research has published clinical guidelines for the illnesses and conditions listed below. You can get consumer or practitioner-oriented details from AHCPR's Web site (www.ahcpr.gov) or by calling 800-358-9295:

Acute pain management

Acute low back problems

Pressure ulcers in adults

Post-stroke rehabilitation

Cataracts in adults

Cardiac rehabilitation

Depression in primary care

Smoking cessation

Sickle-cell disease hyperplasia

Benign prostatic

Otitis media (ear infection)

Management of cancer

Heart failure with effusion

Unstable angina

Pain

through classes or one-on-one sessions rather than just written materials—the better. Find out if a program's goal is to teach you how to manage your own condition. This so-called self-care management approach doesn't work for every condition, but it has helped many people regain a sense of autonomy and a level of daily functioning that had been beyond reach. Halsted Holman, a professor at Stanford University's medical school and director of the Stanford Arthritis Center in Palo Alto, California, has reported on significant improvements resulting from a self-care program for arthritis suffers which has boosted patients' well-being and mobility while also reducing costs. The process involves teaching patients how to "be masters over their disease," says Fama. Then the masters become the leaders who teach another group of sufferers how to prevail.

The last hurdle for an HMO's disease management program: are the plan's docs following the guidelines? It's one thing to say on a piece of paper that your program hews to a treatment blueprint. It's quite another to get your doctors to actually do it. Tracking doctors' behavior in these disease areas is one way for an HMO to hold them accountable. If you find an HMO that records doctors' adherence to guidelines, you've probably found a plan that's truly committed to providing top-notch care in that area. It should be able to give you an actual record of its success along many dimensions, such as hospitalization or procedure rates, patient satisfaction, and family satisfaction.

DO distinguish between good and bad case management.

IN AN IDEAL HMO, you wouldn't have to do your own research on your disease or illness, lobby for referrals to specialists, coordinate community services to help with your disability, and communicate the findings of one medical professional to another. Instead, you'd have a case manager who would do all that and more. Many disease management programs use case management techniques, but they're not the same thing. An HMO that doesn't have a special program for your condition may nevertheless have a case management program, which members with very complicated conditions may be eligible for. HMOs have been practicing case management for years, but their effectiveness varies greatly.

The first characteristic you should look for is a "high intensity" case management program, as described by Drs. James Pacala and Chad Boult, geriatricians and health services researchers at the University of Minnesota who studied case management programs at 23 HMOs. Ask the HMO to answer these questions:

◆ **Does case management apply to members who are outpatients?** Most management services are concentrated on hospitalized members. You'll be more likely to benefit if the HMO also puts a significant number of outpatients into a case management program.

◆ **What's the ratio of members to case managers?** In high-intensity programs, managers—typically nurses or social workers—carry small case loads of 40 members or fewer. "If someone says they have a ratio of 110 patients to 1 case manager, that's not really case management," says Fama.

◆ **How much time will I spend with my case manager?** In high-intensity programs, managers spend at least half their time in direct client contact.

◆ **How is a care plan formulated?** Most managers craft a plan for your care after your health and functioning is assessed. Look for a care plan that is fashioned only after consulting with the patient and with a multidisciplinary team. In eight of the HMOs studied by the University of Minnesota, case managers arranged for services without conferring with the patient and without establishing goals.

In low-intensity programs, case management looks a lot more like cost management, something that benefits the HMO, but isn't necessarily advancing members' best interests. In such systems, case managers rarely have face-to-face contact with members and spend most of their time on the telephone arranging services which are provided by someone else.

DON'T assume you'll get a case manager.

IF YOU FEEL YOUR BEST BET for improving or maintaining your condition is to get into the case management program, you'll need to understand how to do it. The obvious question: Can you simply request case management? While some 61 percent of the HMOs studied by the University of Minnesota team accepted these so-called family referrals, only a small proportion of the patients in case management landed there as a result of a family referral. Will the extremity of your case help you get in? Astonishingly, it may not. Most HMOs draft members into case management on the basis of physician recommendations, a fairly random process. "It is striking how few of the programs we surveyed have anything approaching a systematic mechanism for identifying and screening potential beneficiaries," reported Pacala and Boult. What that means is that there's no clear way to figure out if you'll get into the program. If an HMO uses doctor referrals alone to move patients into case management, you're stuck with trying to find the doctors whose recommendations carry the most weight.

HMOs which use several methods of screening and target your "diagnostic group" will probably give you a better chance of getting into the program. The most commonly targeted diagnostic groups among Medicare HMOs are congestive heart failure, chronic obstructive pulmonary disease, diabetes, stroke, cancer, and members who are heavy users of services. Other screening methods include the site

CASE MANAGEMENT: HOW GOOD IS IT?

CASE MANAGEMENT IS a phrase HMOs love to lay claim to. To someone who's chronically sick it sounds heavenly—someone within the faceless bureaucracy who knows how to improve your health, organize your appointments, and be your advocate. In theory, case management does all that and more. But in practice, case management may fall short. Here are the findings of a University of Minnesota study of 18 Medicare HMOs with more than 20,000 members, as well as five other health plans:

◆ **Caseloads vary dramatically.** How much attention you receive depends on how many other squeaky wheels your case manager has to deal with. Fourteen percent of plans reported that case managers had fewer than 20 patients, while 17 percent said each of their managers were shouldering more than 120 patients.

◆ **Some HMOs phone it in.** Any intervention on your behalf is probably better than nothing, but there's a big difference in how well case managers get to know you at different HMOs. A slim majority—61 percent—include home visits in their programs. The rest intervene only by phone.

◆ **Outside help fluctuates.** Most chronic needs should be tackled on all fronts: physical, social, emotional, and spiritual. You can't expect all that from an HMO, but good case management programs try to address all dimensions by arranging for community-based services that aren't covered by your plan. Some 65 percent of the programs helped coordinate outside support in this way.

of care, in which admission to a hospital or nursing home triggers case management for a member; limited function; age; and a member's living circumstances.

THE CUTTING EDGE

WHO'S WORKING HARDEST TO RAISE the level of care given to chronic care HMO members? One way to judge may be by tapping into the National Chronic Care Consortium's Web site (www.ncccresourcecenter.org/default.html). Though it's designed for hospitals, doctors, and health plans, the site could help you identify leaders in chronic care. Check out NCCC's sample issue of *CareLink,* a monthly publication for subscribers, and its page of links to other sites dedicated to chronic conditions.

How Expensive Are You?
Most HMOs make money by keeping a tight lid on costs. You, or a chronically ill family member, are a budget buster. Medical costs for persistent conditions are two to nearly six times as high as outlays for a one-time illness.

1987 PER CAPITA MEDICAL COSTS

Acute condition only	$817
One chronic condition	$1,829
More than one chronic condition	$4,672

DO study the HMO's referral system.

IF YOU'RE NOT IN A CASE management program, it'll be up to you to find and see the specialists you need. Since getting referrals to specialists is one of the biggest complaints consumers have had about HMOs, it's worth putting some time into assessing how difficult it is. Most HMOs ask their primary care doctors to be the gatekeepers who say yea or nay to consultations with a specialist. Find out if the doctor is penalized—financially or otherwise—for referring patients to too many specialists. Ask what the doctor has to go through with the HMO's administration to actually grant you a referral. The HMO should answer these

Where Does the Money Go?

Most of the money spent on chronic conditions is consumed by hospitals and doctors administering care during difficult episodes. More preventive or rehabilitative spending would be better.

MEDICAL COSTS FOR PEOPLE WITH CHRONIC CONDITIONS

Hospital	39%
Physician	25%
Other*	24%
Nursing Home	12%

*INCLUDING PRESCRIPTIONS, DENTAL CARE, HOME HEALTH, MEDICAL EQUIPMENT, NONPHYSICIAN PRACTITIONERS (1990, $425 BILLION)

SOURCE (FOR BOTH TABLES): HOFFMAN, CATHERINE AND RICE, DOROTHY P. ESTIMATES BASED ON THE 1987 NATIONAL MEDICAL EXPENDITURE SURVEY. UNIVERSITY OF CALIFORNIA, SAN FRANCISCO— INSTITUTE FOR HEALTH AND AGING, 1995.
SOURCE FOR NURSING HOME COSTS: LETSCH, SW, LAZENBY, HC, LEVIT, KR, COWAN, CA. "NATIONAL HEALTH EXPENDITURES, 1991." HEALTH CARE FINANCING REVIEW, WINTER 1992, 14(2):1-30, TABLE 14

questions, but it's worth seeking out some doctors in the HMO for an even clearer picture. In a move that makes terrific sense for folks with chronic conditions, many plans such as Connecticare in Farmington, Connecticut, and Oxford Health Plans of Stamford, Connecticut, have begun allowing members to select a specialist as their primary care doctor.

PROFILE 4

RETIREES

THIS IS A TIME OF TREMENDOUS flux for senior health care. Because Medicare is scheduled to go bust unless fiscal problems are fixed, the U.S. government is anxious to channel seniors into managed care's cost-conscious arena. But managed care's record with seniors is short and spotty. Yes, Medicare HMOs offer vision care, pharmacy, and other welcome benefits that aren't available under traditional Medicare. And it's true that they can be an excellent and inexpensive option for healthy seniors. But there are some arresting concerns that are only beginning to be addressed by HMOs and the Health Care Financing Administration, which oversees Medicare.

First and foremost, Medicare HMOs have been operating almost without supervision. Until 1993, they weren't required to report information to HCFA. Since 1993, they've been subject to something called "peer" review, which involves a selective audit of patient files and treatment records. But results of the review aren't published, and subpar HMOs aren't kicked out of the Medicare program. Meanwhile, more and more companies are rushing to open Medicare HMOs, and older people are joining them at the rate of 100,000 a month.

Also, as mostly for-profit companies, HMOs are subject to cost squeezes like any other company. Folks who are 65 or older represent 13 percent of the population, but consume 35 cents of every health care dollar spent in this country. Not only do older people cost more, the HMO can't raise its revenue to cover those costs because its pay is dictated by HCFA. What happens when the expenses associated with those attractive pharmacy benefits start escalating? Or when HCFA decides to lower the rate at which it reimburses Medicare HMOs—which a federal advisory panel has recommended that Congress do as soon as possible? "When you start lowering those rates you're lowering the profits. Some of these wonderful extra freebie benefits, such as prescription coverage or free eyeglasses, are going to disappear," predicts Fredda Vladeck, an adviser on aging to the International Brotherhood of Teamsters.

Finally, most Medicare HMOs aren't engineered for the special demands of aging bodies. Their cost-efficient approach calls for one primary physician to handle as many health problems as possible. But the chronically ill elderly benefit more than any other group from a host of specialists putting their heads together and coordinating care. "If the gatekeeper physician is basically the Iron Chancellor, and you have to be threatening a lawsuit to get to see anyone beyond that person, it's not helpful to anything but the HMO's solvency," says Loren Lipson, chief of geriatric medicine at the University of Southern California. Worse, if an HMO attracts a disproportionate number of chronically sick elderly with a first-rate disease management program, it will get itself into financial hot water. "They have a tremendous disincentive to develop good programs for heart disease, stroke patients, and sick people," points out Diane Archer, executive director of the Medicare Rights Center in New York, New York.

Soon these issues will get even more complicated. The budget bill signed by President Clinton in August 1997 allows a handful of new options for Medicare beneficiaries, beginning in 1998. They include:

◆ **Private fee-for-service insurance plans.** Seniors can pay a premium to join a plan that offers the same medical benefits as Medicare, as well as some extras. Such plans would pay doctors more handsomely than traditional Medicare.

◆ **Private contracting with doctors.** This change lets Medicare beneficiaries pay doctors on their own, at any rate the doctor wishes to charge, without filing a Medicare claim.

◆ **Medical saving accounts.** Up to 390,000 seniors will be able to buy a high-deductible insurance policy from the government to cover big-ticket medical expenses and establish a tax-free savings account to cover routine expenses.

◆ **New HMO cousins.** In addition to a point-of-service plan (POS), which allows beneficiaries to pay for some care outside an HMO's network, you will be able to join two other kinds of HMOs: a preferred provider organization (PPO), which gives you some freedom in choosing doctors, and a provider-sponsored organization (PSO), which is a managed care plan run by doctors and hospitals rather than insurance companies.

These new alternatives will eventually allow seniors to fashion the kind of health care that best fits their budget and physical needs. But none of them address the paramount problem: we don't know if Medicare beneficiaries are getting high-caliber care. It's heartening to know that HCFA is clearly committed to holding Medicare HMOs to a higher level of accountability than exists now. But agreeing on measures and reporting requirements will take time. Until regulatory agencies kick into gear, you'll have to work hard to find a Medicare HMO worth joining. Here's how:

DON'T join a plan that doesn't ask questions.

ONE OF THE BEST WAYS a plan can take care of you is to anticipate and minimize your problems before they get worse. How do they do it? They ask you to fill out a questionnaire that tries to identify your health risks. If your Medicare HMO doesn't make an effort to spot high-risk members, look for another one. If it does, judge the questionnaire it uses. The Health Care Financing Administration is now requiring Medicare HMOs to administer something called the SF 36. It's a good sign if an HMO had been using this for some time before the government mandated it. But it's even better if a plan is switching to a newer series of questions called the PraPlus. This survey beats the SF 36 for one very important reason—it actually can predict which members are most likely to have serious problems that could lead to hospitalization. Plans that were beginning to use it in 1997: Oxford Health Plans in

Norwalk, New York; Humana Health Plan in Chicago; Sierra Health Services in Las Vegas; and Prudential in one of its studies. Blue Cross Blue Shield Association has also recommended it to its Medicare HMOs.

Though the PraPlus seems to be a particularly good tool, many HMOs use other surveys. The key is that they discover what your health and social situation is. "It's a good indication that a plan is trying to be proactive," explains Chronic Care Initiative's Fama.

DO look for a holistic approach.

PREVENTIVE EFFORTS OF AN HMO should take on a whole new intensity for the senior population. "The more aggressive the plan is in taking care of things early, the less chance of them becoming intractable," says University of Southern California's Lipson. Moreover, extra vigilance in reducing excess weight and encouraging other healthful behaviors in your later years can improve your quality of life and functioning dramatically. Thus, your game plan should be to broadly assess the plan's preventive endeavors in two realms: what it does to detect disease and illness early and what it does to encourage and maintain healthful behaviors.

In the first category, the HMO should offer free prostrate, colon, breast, and lung cancer screenings regularly, in addition to regular health checkups. Members with heart disease should have easy access to cardiac rehabilitation services. Any HMO that falls short in detecting problems should be passed over. The next category is where you'll find the greatest variability: assessments. Find a plan that will regularly assess your hearing and eyesight (the most common reason people over 65 visit doctors is vision problems). Look also for a plan that scrutinizes members for early signs of depression and dementias. Treatment programs should include support for both members and their caregivers, as well as links to community support groups. Additionally, a Medicare HMO should offer well-developed educational programs in medications, smoking cessation, weight and cholesterol reduction, and other health issues. Ask what kind of follow-up the HMO pursues with class members and how successfully they change behaviors. Excellent Medicare HMOs also offer a range of exercise programs or inducements to exercise. Some, such as Intergroup of Arizona, subsidize membership in a health club that has medical staff on site to monitor members.

DON'T go for the biggest drug freebie.

Pharmacy benefits are a huge lure to most people because traditional Medicare doesn't pay for drugs, yet medications are a tremendous financial drain. It's not uncommon for an older person to take 15 to 20 different medications. An HMO that says it will give you a $500 annual prescription benefit sounds like a fabulous one to join.

But drugs—and drug benefits—are a terrifically complicated issue for seniors. Many drugs simply don't work the same way in an old body as they do in a younger one. Trials of new drugs didn't begin including people up to age 75 until fairly recently. So many drugs that are prescribed to seniors are the result of guesswork, not science. Tagamet, a drug that will alleviate ulcer symptoms in a 40-year-old, for example, is especially likely to interact unpredictably with other drugs or health conditions. It would rarely be appropriate for an 80-year-old, says Pat Wilson, a drug benefit consultant at Wilson & Associates, in Rosemont, Pennsylvania. Twenty percent of Medicare beneficiaries who are hospitalized are admitted because they are taking the wrong combinations of drugs or because they've forgotten to take the medication altogether, according to Lipson.

So a pharmacy benefit that simply subsidizes your medication expenses is not enough. What you really want is one that is also smart about the drugs you take. Not many are. But here are the features of an ideal pharmaceutical plan:

◆ **An electronic dispensing record.** The HMO should capture every drug you're taking in an electronic file that's checked when a new prescription is filled. Will their system attempt to stop any prescription that's being refilled early or that's a duplicate or prescribed by a different doctor? Most pharmacy benefit managers, who run the drug dispensary for plans, will say they do this. Does the file also check one drug's characteristics against others being taken? Analyze the drug relative to the patient's age?

There is a list of drugs that will not be prescribed to anyone over the age of 65 because they're killers among the elderly. Here are 20 medicines—called "killer drugs" by Wilson—that the Government Accounting Office deemed inappropriate for the elderly in a 1995 report (generic names are in parentheses): Valium (Diazepam), Librium (Chlordiazepoxide), Dalmane (Flurazepam), Equanil (Meprobamate), Nembutal (Pentobarbital), Seconal (Secobarbital), Elavil (Amitriptyline), Indocin (Indomethacin), Butazolidin (Phenylbutazone), Diabinese (Chlorpropamide), Darvon (Propoxyphene), Talwin (Pentazocine), Vasodilan (Isoxsuprine), Cyclospasmol (Cyclandelate), Persantine (Dipyridamole), Flexeril (Cyclobenzaprine), Robaxin (Methocaramol), Soma (Carisoprodol), Norflex (Orphenadrine), and Tigan (Trimethobenzamide).

◆ **An electronic patient profile.** This is simply a little file of characteristics on every member that can be checked by any of the plan's pharmacies to see if a drug is suitable. The more information it contains, the better: age, sex, height, weight, bone size, abdominal fat, health conditions, drug allergies, and medications currently being taken. A really sophisticated system would contain family histories and hereditary

dispositions. Will you find this? It will be tough. Pat
Wilson says the best system she knows of is operated
by a tiny company in Jackson Hole, Wyoming, called
APB America.

◆ **A dispensary with a broad list of drugs.** In a tactic that comes uncomfortably close to bait-and-switch
salesmanship, many HMOs offer an appealingly generous drug benefit to draw you into the plan, and
then fall short when it comes time to deliver. How?
Their pharmacy doesn't offer the precise drug you
take. Instead, it carries a substitute or cousin medication that is supposed to accomplish the same
thing. Given the intricacy with which one drug may
interact with another, such substitutions shouldn't be
accepted lightly. Instead, go with a pharmacy that
actually carries your specific medications even if your
out-of-pocket costs are higher. Also find out what
happens if the dispensary drops your drug. Will it
give you a discount if you purchase the drug else-
where? Will it make special acquisitions of medications if requested? Another key question: how long
will the plan guarantee its prescription subsidy? Wilson predicts many prescription benefits won't stand
the test of time. She's seen HMOs whose pharmaceutical benefits shot up 25 percent in 1996. "They'll
have to skinny down the benefits," she says. "It would
be suicide if they didn't."

Notice that the amount of money the plan is willing to pay for your medications is not on this list.
The integrity and sophistication of its pharmacy benefit is much more important to your well-being.
Money should be the last feature you look at in comparing plans.

DO demand drug reviews.

DOCTORS MAY HAVE HAD a pharmacy course or two
in medical school. But chances are that was the sum
total of their drug education, and it was a long time

ago. "They don't intend to do harm, but they don't know which drugs are problematic," says Wilson. Just because an elderly person has taken a medication for 20 years is no reason to keep prescribing it. His or her body has changed, and the drug may no longer be appropriate. Another tricky component doctors often don't master is the fuzzy line between side effects and the aging process. Confusion, forgetfulness, loss of balance, instability of gait may be accepted by many doctors as a natural part of getting older. But those

GRIPE RATE

DURING 1995, SOME 3,151 Medicare HMO members complained about their health plan. These weren't ordinary complaints. They were federal complaints, which means the members had already gone through at least two levels of appeals inside the HMO. While that number was down from 3,271 from the year before, despite higher HMO enrollment, there was a wide disparity among complaint rates. By requesting complaint data under the Freedom of Information Act, *The Wall Street Journal* unearthed the records of some of the largest Medicare HMOs:

HEALTH PLAN	COMPLAINT RATE PER 1,000 MEMBERS
Aetna (S. California)	3.88
Humana (FL)	2.65
PacifiCare (Los Angeles)	1.33
FHP (CA)	1.29
Share/Medica (Minneapolis)	1.09
Kaiser (S. California)	.61
Health Net (N. California)	.56
H.I.P. (NY)	.45
Group Health (Puget Sound)	.30
Oxford (NY)	.28
All U.S.	1.29

infirmities could be resulting from poor drug combinations. A semiannual review of all medications being taken, including over-the-counter drugs, is an ideal way to correct such problems. Find out if the plan you're considering provides this.

DON'T join a Johnny-come-lately.

ONE OF THE WONDERFUL THINGS about a Medicare HMO is that it sounds like it's tailored for older people like you. In fact, most Medicare HMOs are indistinguishable from regular HMOs. The difference is that they met the government's qualifications for opening up a Medicare HMO with the government. Those qualifications? They have at least 5,000 members in this plan, draw at least 50 percent of their members from outside of Medicare and Medicaid programs, and are doctors and hospitals that meet Medicare standards, among other things. It may be tempting to join a new HMO because it may be offering the best incentives, like a car dealer. But restrain yourself. A Medicare HMO is under no obligation to keep operating, and if business conditions sour or the HMO has expanded too quickly, your brand new Medicare HMO can simply close its doors.

You're better off with a longer-established and stable HMO which has served Medicare beneficiaries for five years or more. Because members of Medicare HMOs can quit their plan at any time, to return to traditional Medicare or join another plan, members' quit rate is an especially valid indicator of satisfaction or dissatisfaction. If this rate, called the "disenrollment" rate, is 15 percent or higher, it's a sign of trouble. As with regular HMOs, not-for-profit Medicare plans seem to serve their members better. In a study conducted by Public Citizens' Health Research Group, in Washington, D.C., in 1995, patients in for-profit HMOs were almost five times more likely to file an appeal than patients in not-for-profit plans.

DO demand old-age experts.

IF YOU READ THE DISEASE and case management sections earlier in this chapter, you understand the importance of coordinating many disciplines for chronically ill people. As a senior you should search high and low for a Medicare HMO that not only excels in such coordination but includes specialists not normally found in an HMO: geriatricians, social workers, financial advisers, dietitians, physical thera-

GET THE GOODS ON MEDICARE HMOs

THERE ARE A NUMBER OF ADDITIONAL sources of information on specific plans or fonts of advice you should consider consulting:

◆ *Health Pages* **magazine,** based in New York City, produces special issues which compare managed care plans in a particular region. In 1995 it evaluated Medicare HMOs in three areas: Phoenix, South Florida, and Pittsburgh. In 1996, it published information on St. Louis and Denver. Call 212-505-0103 for more information.

◆ **Local area offices on aging.** Usually found under the department of health and human services in the blue pages, these can often convey useful details about specific HMOs you may be considering.

◆ **State departments of corporations or insurance.** HMOs usually fall under these agencies' jurisdiction. While the complaint and solvency information they collect is very uneven, you might want to check that the HMO you're considering joining isn't the one getting the greatest number of complaints per 1,000 members.

◆ **The Health Insurance Counseling and Advocacy Programs.** These are government-sponsored advicegivers. Call 800-677-1116 for a contact in your area.

◆ **The Medicare Rights Center.** Offers free-of-charge counseling and advocacy on Medicare and Medicare HMOs (212-869-3850).

pists. "There are multiple needs at a time when an older person is going through a devaluation of work and having financial insecurity while the body's systems are deteriorating," explains Lipson.

One example of a program that is specially designed for seniors is SCAN Health Plan, a social Medicare HMO in Long Beach, California, that is part of a demonstration program by HCFA. The goal is to maintain frail elderly in their homes for as long as possible. Usually when a Medicare beneficiary cannot perform one, two, or three activities of daily living, an HMO does little to maintain the member in his or her home. This is a characteristic shortcoming of both traditional Medicare and Medicare HMOs. In contrast, SCAN has a social worker specializing in geriatrics assess frail oldsters when they first enter the program, and then custom-tailors a variety of services—many of them based in the community—according to their needs. Services might include meal deliveries, respite care for spouses, adult day care, and personal care, as well as homemaking. "It's been proven that through the application of a basket of services not offered in traditional Medicare, we can avoid or delay institutionalization," says Stuart Byer, SCAN's vice president of public affairs. SCAN operates two other social HMOs: Kaiser Permanente Center for Health Research, in Portland, Oregon, and Elderplan in Brooklyn, New York. Though Congress has yet to authorize programs countrywide, HCFA has awarded contracts to begin similar programs in Costa Contra County, California; Columbia, South Carolina; Grand Junction, Colorado; and Worcester, Massachusetts.

DON'T forget to consult HCFA.

STARTING IN 1997, HCFA began requiring Medicare HMOs to start stepping up to the plate in terms of reporting requirements. The plans had to convey their HEDIS measures and begin measuring their members' health status and satisfaction. Good HMOs were already doing this, but the HCFA rules mean that you'll be able to make some comparisons. Once again, you should understand that HEDIS data is unaudited, meaning no one is checking that the plans are being scrupulous about their numbers. Moreover, "plans are using different methodologies to collect the data. So even if they're collecting the data accurately, you still can't make an apples-to-apples comparison," cautions Diane Archer, of the Medicare Rights Center in New York, New York. Still, HCFA's organizing of HEDIS, satisfaction, and benefits information in an Internet database in late 1997 will be extremely useful.

HCFA also periodically sanctions HMOs for a variety of reasons. So-called intermediate sanctions apply if a Medicare HMO fails to provide medically necessary services (with adverse results for members), charges enrollees more than it is supposed to, fails to promptly pay claims, or misrepresents information to an individual or to HCFA. In 1996, for example, Blue Cross Blue Shield of Massachusetts was sanctioned and its enrollment frozen for overstating the number of doctors in its plan. An internal compliance effort uncovered the falsification, and the plan itself reported the error to HCFA. Other penalties include suspension of payments to the plan, halting the plan's marketing activities, or refusal to renew an HMO's contract—though the HCFA has rarely doled out this last punishment.

How can you find out if the HMO you're considering has ever been sanctioned? The Department of Health and Human Services' Office of Inspector General (which is responsible for disciplining all Medicare providers who break the rules) used to mail out its Cumulative Sanctions Report until requests for it reached 10,000 per month. Now the only place to check if an HMO has been chastised is to visit the Inspector General's home page (www.sba.gov/

ignet/internal/hhs/hhs.html). Click on Office of Enforcement and Compliance Reports.

TOP FIVE NONHOSPITAL SERVICES

For Adults (65+ years)

SERVICE	NUMBER OF OCCURRENCES
Eye exam	14.3 million
Electrocardiogram	6.9 million
Tonometry (test of eye tension)	5.6 million
Miscellaneous manual examinations and measurements	5.5 million
Removal of lesion or skin through cryosurgery, laser or other means	5.3 million

MOST COMMON HOSPITAL PROCEDURES

For Men (over 64 years)

SERVICE	NUMBER OF OCCURRENCES
Prostatectomy	77,678
Left heart catheterization	66,474
Angioplasty	63,506
Biopsy of esophagus, stomach, or duodenum	47,913
Removal of inner layer of an artery (head and neck)	39,496

MOST COMMON HOSPITAL PROCEDURES

For Women (over 64 years)

SERVICE	NUMBER OF OCCURRENCES
Pins in broken thighbone	73,305
Biopsy of esophagus, stomach, or duodenum	72,268
Total knee replacement	70,749
Left heart catheterization	68,344
C.A.T. scan of head	55,924

CHAPTER

5

ONE OF THE most astonishing shortcomings of our medical system is how little information we have about doctors. In both the old fee-for-service organizations and the new managed care complexes, the medical establishment keeps an iron grip on facts that any reasonable person would want to know about a doctor: Has she been sanctioned by a hospital? For what reasons? Has he been sued for malpractice? How many times? How does that compare to his peers' record? This data is just a fraction of what we really have a right to know, but it's a crucial fraction because it could keep us out of the hands of an incompetent. "Someone who's very charismatic could be in big trouble within the medical community and no one on the outside would ever know it," says Bill Copeland, a consultant who formerly was CEO

of the Pennsylvania operation of United HealthCare, based in Minneapolis, Minnesota.

I believe we are on the cusp of a major breakthrough in getting such vital data and more. New York, Massachusetts, and Florida have begun releasing board-discipline, hospital-sanction, and malpractice statistics on physicians. HMOs are becoming more and more sophisticated about credentialing their doctors—and, slowly, about conveying key pieces of doctor-specific information to their members. Finally, and most importantly, doctors themselves will soon begin shifting their medical record-keeping from written to electronic form. "The profession and the industry are basically years behind. They're in the information business, yet still in the quill and parchment phase in collecting information," says Dr. Alan R. Zwerner, president and CEO of the Medical Quality Commission, an accreditor of physician practices based in Seal Beach, California. Computerization means that the details on a doctor's contact with patients—everything from immunizations to her protocol for treating cardiac patients—will eventually be easily collected, analyzed, and compared to HMO-wide averages.

I don't expect the medical world to bare its soul on these matters without a struggle. The main argument against releasing death rates of cardiac surgeons and other telling statistics is that consumers won't know how to interpret them. This is the kind of patronizing rationale that we used to hear from car companies who didn't want to release crash-testing results and other safety information. It's simply not true. Consumers, not to mention entrepreneurs and publishers, will scramble to find a way to give the information a meaningful context once it's available.

In the meantime, however, here we are with very little in the way of hard data. You can't give short shrift to your doctor hunt even if you've been exhaustive in your HMO selection. Why? The best doctor in the worst HMO is better for your family's health than the worst doctor in the best HMO. Some experts even advise picking your HMO on the basis of the doctor you want to be treated by—essentially making HMO selection secondary to choosing a physician. I'm not adverse to that approach as long as you recognize that your doctor or his HMO could end their relationship, leaving you stuck with the HMO. I don't advise automatically following your old doctor to whichever

HMO he or she affiliates with for the same reason. Unless your relationship is especially close or your physical condition particularly complex, you may be better off with a new doctor in another HMO.

Your research should have three stages. First, make sure the doctors you're considering have no strikes against them, such as disciplinary actions or a large number of complaints. Second, assess the doctors' education, training, and professional reputation. Finally, evaluate each doctor personally, through an interview. Here are the detailed instructions for finding your HMO doctor:

DO look for a board-certified doctor.

LOTS OF PEOPLE POOH-POOH the significance of board certification for a number of reasons. It doesn't necessarily mean a doctor is an ace with patients, highly skilled, or even up-to-date on treatments and procedures. All of this is actually true: Board certification is no guarantee of any of those qualities. It simply means that a doctor has completed a residency approved by a board and then passed the board's exam. But because any doctor with a license can practice any kind of medicine without special training, it's worth looking for a board-certified doctor. Then you can be sure that the doctor was at least trained and supervised in the specialty and proved her competence on an exam.

Still, not all board certificates are equally meaningful. The American Osteopathic Association consists of 17 boards governing 33 medical sectors. The American Board of Medical Specialties contains 24 boards covering 25 specialties ranging from allergy and immunology to urology. The tests given by some boards aren't particularly rigorous. For example, to be certified by the American Board of Colon and Rectal Surgery, doctors must answer 100 multiple-choice questions. In contrast, to obtain certification from the

THE CERTIFICATION TEST

FINDING A BOARD-CERTIFIED DOCTOR among your HMO's physicians shouldn't be too hard—more and more HMOs are requiring their doctors to take the exam and become certified. But some boards grant certification less readily than others. And while some boards require certified doctors to prove their competence again by being periodically retested, others do not. To compare how tough different boards are, check the following list. To find out if a doctor is certified by the American Board of Medical Specialties, call 847-491-9091. The American Osteopathic Association (312-280-7445) no longer responds to certification inquiries over the phone. To find out if a doctor is certified, send $25 to 142 East Ontario, Chicago, IL, 60611, along with a release form signed by the doctor.

SPECIALTY	RECERTIFICATION REQUIREMENTS
AMERICAN BOARD OF MEDICAL SPECIALTIES	
Allergy & Immunology 215-349-9466	Yes, every 10 years. (Docs certified prior to 1989 not required to recertify.)
Anesthesiology 919-881-2570	No
Colon & Rectal Surgery 313-282-9400	No
Dermatology 313-874-1088	Yes, every 10 years. (Docs certified prior to 1991 not required to recertify.)
Emergency Medicine 517-332-4800	Yes, every 10 years.

SPECIALTY	RECERTIFICATION REQUIREMENTS
Family Practice 606-269-5626	Yes, every 7 years.
Internal Medicine 215-243-1500	Yes, every 10 years. (Docs certified prior to 1990 not required to recertify.)
Medical Geriatrics 301-571-1825	No
Neurological Surgery 713-790-6015	No
Nuclear Medicine 310-825-6787	Yes, every 10 years. (Docs certified prior to 1992 not required to recertify.)
Obstetrics & Gynecology 214-871-1619	Yes, every 10 years. (Docs certified prior to 1986 not required to recertify.)
Ophthalmology 215-664-1175	Yes, every 10 years. (Docs certified prior to 1992 not required to recertify.)
Orthopaedic Surgery 919-929-7103	Yes every 10 years. (Docs certified prior to 1985 not required to recertify.)
Otolaryngology 713-528-6200	No

(continued)

THE CERTIFICATION TEST

SPECIALTY	RECERTIFICATION REQUIREMENTS
Pathology 813-286-2444	No
Pediatrics 919-929-0461	Yes, every 7 years. (Docs certified prior to 1988 not required to recertify.)
Physical Medicine & Rehabilitation 507-282-1776	Yes, every 10 years. (Docs certified prior to 1993 not required to recertify.)
Plastic Surgery 215-587-9322	No
Preventive Medicine 847-751-1750	Yes, every 10 years. (Docs certified prior to 1998 not required to recertify.)
Psychiatry & Neurology 847-945-7900	Yes, every 10 years. (Docs certified prior to 1994 not required to recertify.)
Radiology 520-790-2900	No, except for Radiation Onc- ology, which requires recerti- fication every 10 years.
Surgery 215-568-4000	Yes, every 10 years. (Docs certified prior to 1976 not required to recertify.)
Thoracic Surgery 847-475-1520	Yes, every 10 years. (Docs certified prior to 1976

SPECIALTY	RECERTIFICATION REQUIREMENTS
	not required to recertify.)
Urology 810-646-9720	Yes, every 10 years. (Docs certified prior to 1985 not required to recertify.)

AMERICAN OSTEOPATHIC BOARDS

Anesthesiology	No
Dermatology	No
Emergency Medicine	Yes, every 10 years. (Docs certified prior to 1994 not required to recertify.)
Family Physicians	No
Internal Medicine	Yes, every 10 years. (Docs certified prior to 1993 not required to recertify.)
Neurology & Psychiatry	Yes, every 10 years. (Docs certified prior to 1996 not required to recertify.)
Obstetrics & Gynecology	No
Ophthalmology & Otorhinolaryngology	No

(continued)

THE CERTIFICATION TEST

SPECIALTY	RECERTIFICATION REQUIREMENTS
Orthopaedic Surgery	Yes, every 10 years. (Docs certified prior to 1994 not required to recertify.)
Pathology	Yes, every 10 years. (Docs certified prior to 1995 not required to recertify.)
Pediatrics	Yes, every 7 years. (Docs certified prior to 1995 not required to recertify.)
Preventive Medicine	Yes, every 10 years. (Docs certified prior to 1994 not required to recertify.)

American Board of Plastic Surgery, a physician takes a 6 ½-hour multiple-choice and true/false exam on day one, followed by an oral exam which is taken over three days. Doctors also have to submit a 12-month case report, which is reviewed, and eight case lists, which the examiners use to test their knowledge.

The other requirement that varies from board to board is whether a doctor must periodically take another exam to be recertified. This is an extremely important point. If no recertification is required, as is the case with the American Osteopathic Board of Family Physicians or the American Board of Surgery, your doctor's board certification is much less meaningful. He may have taken the exam 30 years ago, never kept up with new developments, and never been trained in new procedures. When checking up on a doctor, ask if she is board certified and when certification was

SPECIALTY	RECERTIFICATION REQUIREMENTS
Proctology	No
Radiology	No
Rehabilitation Medicine	Yes, every 7 years. (Docs certified prior to 1995 not required to recertify.)
Special Proficiency in Osteopathic Manipulative Medicine	Yes, every 10 years. (Docs certified prior to 1995 not required to recertify.)
Surgery	No

granted. If her certification is a decade old, ask if she has been recertified. Also, check to see in which specialties board approval means the most. Two Web sites worth checking for details on a doctor's qualifications: the American Medical Association's Physician Select (www.ama-assn.org) and MedSeek's physician directory (www.medseek.com).

DON'T think board-eligible is good enough.

MANY HMOS REPORT THE percentage of doctors who are "board-eligible" instead of those who are certified by a board. The reason: the doctors have fulfilled all training requirements to sit for the exam, say the HMOs, but they just haven't gotten around to actually taking it because the tests are given infrequently. This argument doesn't wash with me. Doctors who have failed the exam once or a dozen times are also board-eligible, but no one should feel comfortable about their competence. The American Board of Internal Medicine uses and recognizes "board-eligible" as a legitimate descriptor, but the other boards don't approve of it.

DO avoid problem doctors.

A DOCTOR HAS TO SCREW UP pretty badly to be disciplined by a state board of medicine or the federal government. But eventually a doctor who overprescribes drugs, abuses alcohol or drugs, or is convicted of criminal activity will be disciplined by having his license suspended, being fined, put on probation, or permanently barred from practicing medicine. Can you find out who they are? Amazingly, it's still not as easy as it should be. The obvious first stop is your state's department of health, board of medical examiners, or other agency that governs doctors. States differ tremendously in what they offer consumers. For example, Indiana and Mississippi won't tell you if a doctor is board certified or describe her education and residency. Michigan can give you education and residency information—but only if you send in a written request under the Freedom of Information Act. Delaware and Minnesota won't convey any information about complaints.

In contrast, New York's State Department of Health issues a monthly report on its disciplinary actions. The listing contains the doctor's name, address, reason for discipline, and the action taken. You can get this report either by calling 518-474-8357 or by visiting its Web site (www.health.state.ny.us). The Rhode Island Department of Health can flood you with information on one of its doctors, including licensing history, board certification, year of certification, disciplinary actions, malpractice coverage, hospital privileges, and residency training (*see pgs. 142–49 for phone numbers and Web sites of state medical boards and departments of health*).

A doctor who hasn't been disciplined by a state may still be practicing in a way that's making patients or colleagues unhappy enough to complain. You can discover if that's the case by calling a local medical society, usually organized by county. "Medical societies don't want to be tarred with bad apples, so if they have complaint information about doctors, they'll give it to you," says Dennis O'Leary, president of the Joint Commission on Accreditation of Healthcare Organizations (JCAHO), an Oakbrook Terrace, Illinois-based accreditor of HMOs, hospitals, group practices, and other health care organizations. You can find your local medical society by calling your state's medical association *(see pgs. 42–48)*.

A truly cautious soul will want to be sure that his or her doctor hasn't been disciplined in any state. For that you need a national directory. The Public Citizens' Health Research Group, a consumer watchdog outfit based in Washington, D.C., publishes *13,012 Questionable Doctors*, a list of doctors disciplined by the states or the federal government. You can order either the three-volume national set ($250) or an edition covering a single state ($15); call 202-588-1000. For more details on the group's findings visit www.citizen. org/hrg. Another one-stop source on dubious practitioners could be the National Practitioner Data Bank, created in 1986 to track health care professionals of all kinds who are disciplined. Unfortunately, for now the 62,000 names are only available to HMOs, hospitals, clinics, and state medical licensing boards.

DON'T simply rely on a friend's opinion.

WHAT'S WRONG WITH ASKING your friends about their doctors? It's what we've all done from time to time—and generally, it works out well. But there's a problem with a neighbor's or a colleague's referral. Unless a friend is a health care professional, she isn't

UNEARTHING PROBLEM DOCS

MOST HMOs MAKE A REASONABLE effort to "credential" their doctors, which means they verify that a doctor is as educated, trained, and licensed as he claims to be. Obviously, they aren't anxious to hire physicians who've been disciplined by the state or federal government. Still, you can double-check if a doctor has been disciplined by calling the state medical board that licenses doctors or the state agency listed below:

Alabama Board of Medical Examiners
P.O. Box 946
Montgomery, AL 36101   334-242-4116

Alaska State Medical Association
P.O. Box 110806
Juneau, AL 99811   907-465-2541

Arizona Board of Medical Examiners
1651 E. Morten Ave., Ste. 210
Phoenix, AZ 85020   602-255-3751

Arkansas State Medical Board
2100 Riverfront Dr., Ste. 200
Little Rock, AR 72202   501-296-1802

California Medical Board
1426 Howe Ave., Ste. 54
Sacramento, CA 95825-3236   916-263-2499

Colorado Board of Medical Examiners
1560 Broadway, Ste. 1300
Denver, CO 80202-5140   303-894-7690

(Connecticut) Department of Public Health and Administration
Licensure and Registration
150 Washington St.
Hartford, CT 06106   860-509-7587

Department of Health Services
Hearing Office   203-566-1011

Board of Medical Practice of Delaware
Division of Professional Regulation
Margaret O'Neill Bldg., 2nd Floor
P.O. Box 1401
Dover, DE 19903   302-739-4522

District of Columbia Board of Medicine
Department of Consumer Affairs
605 G St., Rm. 202LL
Washington, DC 20001   202-727-9794

Florida Board of Medicine
1940 N. Monroe St.   904-488-0595
Tallahassee, FL 32399   www.state.fl.us/fdhc

(Georgia) Composite State Board of Medical Examiners
166 Pryor St. SW
Atlanta, GA 30303   404-656-3913

(Hawaii) Board of Medical Examiners
Professional Vocational Division
P.O. Box 3469
Honolulu, HI 96801   808-586-2708

(continued)

UNEARTHING PROBLEM DOCS

Idaho State Board of Medical Examiners
P.O. Box 83720
Boise, ID 83720-2822   208- 334-2822

Illinois Department of Professional Regulation
320 W. Washington St., 3rd Floor
Springfield, IL 62786   217-785-0820

Medical Licensing Board of Indiana
Health Professions Bureau
Record Division, Rm. 041
402 W. Washington St.
Indianapolis, IN 46204   317-232-2960

Iowa State Board of Medical Examiners
State Capital Complex
Executive Hills West
Des Moines, IA 50319   515-281-5171

Kansas State Board of Healing Arts
235 S. Topeka Blvd.
Topeka, KS 66603   913-296-7413

Kentucky Medical Licensure Board
310 Whittington Pkwy., Ste. 1B
Louisville, KY 40222   502- 429-8046

Louisiana State Board of Medical Examiners
630 Camp St.
New Orleans, LA 70130   504-524-6763

(Maine) Board of Licensure and Medicine
2 Bangor St.
Augusta, ME 04333   207-287-3601

(Maryland) Board of Physician Quality Assurance
4201 Patterson Ave.
Third Floor
Baltimore, MD 21215   410-764-4777

(Massachusetts) Board of Registration in Medicine
10 West St.
Boston, MA 02111   617-727-3086

Michigan Board of Medicine
611 W. Ottawa St.
Box 30018
Lansing, MI 48909   517-335-0918

Minnesota Board of Medical Practice
2700 University Ave., W, Ste. 106
St. Paul, MN 55114   612-617-2130

(Mississippi) State Medical Licensure Board
2688 D Insurance Center Dr.
Jackson, MS 39216   601-354-6645

Missouri State Board of Registration for the Healing Arts
3605 Missouri Blvd., Box 4
Jefferson City, MO 65102   314-751-0098

(Montana) Professional and Occupational Licensing
Board of Medical Examiners
111 N. Jackson, Box 200513
Helena, MT 59620-0513   406-444-4284

(Nebraska) Bureau of Examining Boards
301 Centennial Mall S.
Lincoln, NE 68509-5009   402-471-2115

UNEARTHING PROBLEM DOCS

Nevada State Board of Medical Examiners
P.O. Box 7238
Reno, NV 89510   702-688-2559

New Hampshire Board of Registration in Medicine
2 Industrial Park Dr., Ste. 8
Concord, NH 03301-8520   603-271-1203

(New Jersey) Board of Medical Examiners
140 E. Front St.
Trenton, NJ 08608   609-292-4843

New Mexico Board of Medical Examiners
491 Old Santa Fe Trail
Lamy Bldg., 2nd Floor
Santa Fe, NM 87501   505-827-5022

New York State Department of Health
Corning Tower Empire State Plaza   518-474-8357
Albany, NY 12237   www.health.state.ny.us

New York State Department of Education
Division of Professional Licensing
Albany, NY 12230   518-486-5205

North Carolina Board of Medical Examiners
P.O. Box 20007
Raleigh, NC 27609   919-828-1212

North Dakota State Board of Medical Examiners
City Center Plaza
418 E. Broadway Ave., Ste. 12
Bismarck, ND 58505   701-328-6500

State Medical Board of Ohio
77 S. High St., 17th Floor
Columbus, OH 43266-0315   614-466-3934

Oklahoma State Board of Medical Licensure and Supervision
P.O. Box 18256
Oklahoma City, OK 73154-0256   405-848-6841

(Oregon) Board of Medical Examiners
1500 S.W. 1st Ave., Ste. 620
Portland, OR 97201-5826   503-229-5770

(Pennsylvania) State Board of Medicine
P.O. Box 2649
Harrisburg, PA 17105   717-787-2381

Rhode Island Department of Health
Rhode Island Board of Medical Licensure and Discipline
3 Capitol Hill
Providence, RI 02908   401-277-3855

State Board of Medical Examiners of South Carolina
101 Executive Center Dr.
Saluda Bldg., Ste. 120
P.O. Box 212269
Columbia, SC 29221-2269   803-731-1650

(South Dakota) State Board of Medical and Osteopathic Examiners
1323 S. Minnesota Ave.
Sioux Falls, SD 57105   605-336-1965

(continued)

UNEARTHING PROBLEM DOCS

(Tennessee) Department of Health
Health Related Boards
344 Cordell Hull Bldg.
Nashville, TN 37247   615-532-4384

(Texas) Department of Health
State Board of Medical Examiners
1100 W. 49th St.
Austin, TX 78756   512-305-7010

(Utah) Business Regulation
Division of Occupational and Professional Licensing
160 E. 300 S.
P.O. Box 45805
Salt Lake City, UT 84145   801-530-6733

(Vermont) Secretary of State Office
Board of Medical Practice
109 State St.
Montpelier, VT 05609-1106   802-828-2674

really equipped to evaluate a physician's expertise. Chances are, she'll focus on the doctor's availability, personality, and helpfulness. Those are all useful things to know, but they're not substantive enough to base your decision on. If you're going to ask about a friend's doctor, be pointed about your research questions:

◆**Ask about being sick.** This is when the doctor's skills and responsiveness are most vital. Find out the doctor's course of treatment, alternatives offered to your friend, and the outcome. Does the doctor have an aggressive or conservative approach? How well did the doctor and her office communicate and follow up with the patient?

(Virginia) Board of Medicine
Department of Health Professions
6606 W. Broad St., 4th Floor
Richmond, VA 23230-1717   804-662-9908

(Washington) Department of Health
P.O. Box 47866
Olympia, WA 98504-7866   360-753-2287

West Virginia Board of Medicine
101 Dee Dr.
Charleston, WV 25311   304-558-2921

Wisconsin Medical Examining Board
1400 E. Washington Ave.
P.O. Box 8935
Madison, WI 53708   608-266-2811

Wyoming Board of Medicine
Barrett Bldg., 2nd Floor
Cheyenne, WY 82002   307-778-7053

◆**Ask about hospitalizations and specialists.**
You'd want your primary care doctor to be a powerful advocate and attentive coordinator of any serious problems. Explore every detail of the doctor's involvement and oversight of a hospitalization. Communication with surgeons and specialists is especially important.

An even better way to evaluate a doctor's reputation is to check with his peers. Membership in a local medical society isn't a dramatic sign of approval. Many of them will let any doctor join. Still, it's noteworthy if a doctor doesn't belong to a medical society. "Doctors don't join medical societies for various reasons, but

some don't belong because they aren't good doctors,"
says JCAHO's O'Leary. "On balance, I'd be more
comfortable with someone who's a member of a medical society."

You can get a slightly better picture of a specialist's
reputation among her colleagues by knowing her status in a specialty medical society, such as the American College of Cardiology or the American College of
Rheumatology. Some of these have two levels of membership: basic and fellow status. Basic membership
may not signify anything more than competence,
which of course is desirable. But fellowship status is
much more impressive, because it means a doctor's
experience, accomplishments, and standing among
peers are distinctive.

DO be impressed by accredited doctors' groups.
WHEN NCQA ACCREDITS HEALTH PLANS, it requires
them to prove that they do a good job of verifying
their doctors' educational and training background.
While this credentialing process means that the doctors in our HMOs are more likely to be who they claim
to be, no one should mistake this verification process
for a highly discriminating physician selection system.
The trend today, in fact, is for HMOs to cram as many
doctors as they can on their panels because most consumers seek as broad a choice as possible. Being
selective falls by the wayside. "Some of the large
HMOs have adopted the policy that if there is no bad
information on a doctor, he or she is probably okay,"
says O'Leary.

Doctors' groups themselves can be accredited too,
though. Both the JCAHO and the Medical Quality
Commission, in Seal Beach, California, will evaluate
group practices against quality standards. Accreditation by the JCAHO, which only 15 groups have
obtained, signifies that the doctor group does careful
record-keeping and hews to quality improvement

practices. Some who have been accredited: Ear, Nose and Throat Associates of Rockford, in Rockford, Illinois; Cosmetic and Laser Center in Elmhurst, Illinois; and Garrett Eye Center in Iron Mountain, Michigan. As of mid-1997, only one PPO—USA Managed Care in Austin, Texas—was requiring doctors' groups to be accredited, but the JCAHO expects more plans to move in this direction.

The Medical Quality Commission assesses group practices in 14 areas, also looking for their ability to track patient encounters, collect patient satisfaction data, and act on grievances, among other things. Some of the 30 groups which have earned the commission's accreditation in California include the Scripps Clinic and Foundation in La Joya; Mullikin Medical Centers in Long Beach; Bristol Park Medical Group in Irvine; and HealthCare Partners Medical Group, in Los Angeles. If you can find a doctor in a medical group that has been accredited by either of these organizations, I'd count that heavily in her favor. After all, it's the doctor's office where you really get your care. And though a group accreditation is no guarantee of quality, it shows a commitment to quality and accountability that at this point is very unusual.

Even without accreditation, some group practices are way ahead of HMOs in setting and achieving quality goals. Though it seems far removed from the practice of medicine, a group's ability to collect information, particularly on patient encounters, is a key component of excellence today. The more detail that a group practice can aggregate on how patients are treated, the better it can evaluate its own successes and failures—like any modern-day company. The ability of Tricounty Physicians Association, in Chicago, Illinois, to track such data is so good that it usually has to correct the reports that its HMOs send out to "help" the physicians' association, says Dr. Jeffry Kreamer, TPA's chief executive officer. "But most groups aren't like us. I don't know of any group that has as good control over its information systems."

Group practices that excel in gathering information, especially those few that capture clinical encounters electronically, are likely to be among the best you'll find. Unfortunately, there's no easy way to find out how well a doctor's practice does this except to ask the ones you're considering.

DON'T overlook a doctor's limits.

THERE'S ANOTHER WAY to get a handle on how professionals view a doctor's skills that few consumers know about: learn about what a doctor is officially allowed and not allowed to do at the hospital she's associated with. These limitations are called "clinical privileges." Hospitals have been deciding which doctors can perform which procedures within their walls for decades in order to secure a good reputation and limit their risk. If you discover that one of the doctors you're considering has a broad range of privileges at the most prestigious hospital in your region, and the other has limited privileges at a more modest institution, you have a quick indicator of the confidence that health care professionals have in the two doctors. Ask about a prospective doctor's privileges.

There's one problem with using privileges to assess doctors. Many primary care and other doctors offering ambulatory care aren't on a hospital's staff, so they haven't been rated in this way. "This is what managed care said it was going to do—make sure that the doctor is competent to do what he says he can do. But not too many can," says Charles Jacobs, CEO of InterQual, a developer of software for HMOs.

Though most HMOs don't assign privileges or limits to their doctors, JCAHO's O'Leary believes they soon will. Part of his company's accrediting process requires HMOs to take the first step toward privileging. For example, an HMO doctor who says he can provide obstetric services should have had a residency that included delivering babies. Over the next four years, the privileging information that JCAHO demands from HMOs seeking accreditation will escalate. Check to see if your HMO has established clinical privileges for its doctors or has plans to.

DO check out a doc's hospital associations.

IN THE HIERARCHY OF MEDICINE, teaching hospitals with strong ties to universities are at the top. So, a doctor who completed a residency at University Hospital, a teaching hospital associated with the University of Medicine and Dentistry in Newark, New Jersey, is thought to be better trained than one whose residency was at St. Barnabas in nearby Livingston, New Jersey. Similarly, a doctor who's on staff at a teaching hospital is extremely desirable. Typically, these doctors are leaders who have earned the respect of colleagues. This sort of position reverberates in several ways that can be important to you. First, the doctor will have the full support and attention of the hospital's faculty, staff, and departments. She is also likely to be familiar with experts at other institutions across the country. And, of course, she'll be familiar with the latest research and developments in her field.

But understand a couple of key points about teaching doctors. A professorship is meaningful to you only if it relates to a doctor's area of clinical expertise. Sound obvious? It's possible for a doctor to teach about an area of medicine that isn't related to his practice, and therefore doesn't enhance his service to you. Also, you want to make sure that a doctor's academic title has the word "clinical" in it. That means the professor puts more emphasis on treating patients than on academic research or classroom teaching.

If no teaching doctors are available to you, look for a doctor who is on the medical staff, called an "attending physician," of the best hospital in your area. While the relationships between doctors and hospitals are increasingly governed by economic relationships with HMOs, the best hospitals are still extremely selective and still attracting the best doctors.

DON'T be fooled by referral services.

IT'S NOT THAT YOU CAN'T FIND a good doctor from your local hospital's referral service. You can. But you have to do the same homework you'd do on any other doctor. A hospital's referral service doesn't distinguish between one doctor's skill and reputation and another's. Usually, the service has hundreds of names and hands out two or three to you based on where you live. To give all doctors an equal chance at obtaining new patients, the names are usually rotated. So, if your neighbor called right after you, she'd likely be given the next two or three names on the list. Other referral services are similarly undiscriminating, usually listing any doctor who applies or pays a small fee to be included on the roster.

DON'T assume you can see every doc in the directory.

THE DETAILS PROVIDED BY HMO directories of doctors are usually extremely unhelpful. But even worse, the directory itself may be inaccurate or misleading. As all too many HMO members have learned, not all of the doctors listed are really at your disposal. Here are the reasons why:

◆ **The doctor may have dropped out.** HMOs don't update their directories every time a doctor decides to drop his contract with the plan or stops accepting new patients from the HMO for a period of time. Call to check that the doctor is still working with an HMO.

◆ **The plan may have dropped the doctor.** Directories also get stale because of HMO-initiated changes. Some HMOs put as many doctors as they can on their list, in order to attract members. But once members have joined, the plans whittle down their doctor list for financial reasons. Make sure the annual turnover rate for doctors at an HMO is not more than 10 percent for the last two or three years.

◆ **Not all of the doctors are meant for you.** This is the trickiest surprise in a directory. You'd naturally assume that you're free to see any doctor in an HMO's directory. But in fact, the list is subdivided according to where you live. So while you may be given a list of doctors in New Jersey, New York, and Connecticut, if you live in New Jersey you're only free to see the physicians who practice there. Similarly, invisible boundaries for specialists, subspecialists, and hospitals in the directory may exist. Find out which are really available to you.

◆ **Much of your care won't come from doctors.** HMOs and their doctors increasingly use nurses and physician's assistants for patient care. This isn't necessarily a bad thing. It simply means that the doctor's role may be more limited than you expect. Licensed nurse practitioners are nurses who've had extra training beyond that needed for a nursing license. They, not your doctor, may be the ones who conduct a physical exam, order a diagnostic test, and diagnose your illness. Find out how when and why a doctor's practice will use such "mid-level practitioners" and decide if you're comfortable with that.

DO interview a prospective doctor.

THIS IS A LOT HARDER THAN it sounds. First, you have to make the time and effort. Second, you have to find doctors who are willing to do the same. Unfortunately, many aren't. And others will foist you off onto their office staff. Aim for a face-to-face session with a doctor, but settle for a telephone interview if you must. While the point of this interview is primarily to gauge your chemistry with a physician, you'll get a more comprehensive feeling for each doctor's style if your questions cover a broad set of issues. Here are some suggested questions:

◆ How much experience do you have with my (or my family's) particular health issues?

◆ How much of a role do you think patients should take in deciding on a course of action?

◆ What are your feelings about alternatives to traditional medicine?

◆ Does this HMO allow you to practice the best medicine you can?

◆ Does this HMO penalize you financially or otherwise for ordering tests or referring patients to specialists?

◆ Can you create a comprehensive plan (including nutrition, exercise, and preventive measures) for improving my health?

CHAPTER

6

Getting the
Most
OUT OF YOUR PLAN

F HMOS WERE EVERYTHING they should be, this chapter wouldn't be necessary. You could look at your member handbook, understand your benefits, and get the care you need—when you need it. Unfortunately, it isn't that simple. The old health care system encouraged too much care, and the new one errs on the side of providing too little care. The old system helped doctors act as your advocate and champion. The new system often penalizes them for doing so. So even if you have taken great pains to choose the best plan and the best doctor you possibly can, your job is not done. Until state and federal legislation and other checks and balances are put into place, you must be the one to ensure you get the best out of your plan.

You can figure out the easy stuff. You know that you should understand your benefits and

take advantage of them by getting the annual physical, attending educational sessions on topics that concern you, and using the HMO's free or low-cost preventive services. In this chapter I will focus on the difficulties you may face and strategies to use when you find yourself thwarted by your plan. While it's easy to slip into a defensive, adversarial posture toward your HMO, I hope that you'll aim for a more fundamental shift in perspective, from a passive recipient of medical care to a savvy consumer of health care services. This will be the biggest favor you can do for yourself and your family. The more informed and assertive we become about the medical care we're receiving, the faster health plans will respond to our demands. And taking responsibility for one's own health and healing has also long been considered one of the key elements in getting the best outcomes.

Below you'll find steps and strategies to help you become a more effective consumer. The next chapter will focus on additional issues that pertain to members of Medicare HMOs, as well as the legal options you might consider if all else fails.

DO start a medical log.

THE FIRST STEP IN TAKING CHARGE of our health care is to pay attention to it. Sounds simple, and you may feel you already do this through diet, exercise, and other health-enhancing habits. What I'm suggesting is that you be just as attentive in another area: your interactions with your health plan. You should keep an ongoing record of your doctor visits, medications, referrals, tests, and preventive screenings for two reasons. First, it'll give you a better understanding of your own health. It will help in simple ways, by reminding you of the name of the prescription drug that finally proved effective against your daughter's cold sores. And it could help you solve larger health problems. If you have a vague gastrointestinal problem that manifests itself occasionally, and for which you've consulted different doctors, a medical log may help you see a pattern over the years that no one else can see because no one else has *all* of your medical records in one place. Or, your register could help you tell the next doctor you consult about this problem which treatments have been tried and failed. "Managed care has fragmented doctor-patient relationships so much that now there's hardly any one place where all the information is available on the patient," says Dr. Vincent Riccardi, president of American Medical Consumers, an independent patient advocate service based in La Crescenta, California.

The other reason to keep a record is that, somewhere down the line, you may need to document the care and services you've received. If you ever formally challenge a health plan's decision, your chronicle will be a key factor in a review of your situation. No one should approach their relationship with their doctor or health plan with an adversarial attitude. But if a dispute should arise, and your opinion of what happens differs from what a doctor recalls, you won't have anything to fall back upon unless you make such notes.

At a minimum, your health diary should contain three kinds of information. First, enter and periodically update your vital statistics, such as blood type, weight, blood pressure, blood chemistry results, chronic aches and pains, and other information that comes from any tests or screenings. The second, most important part of your log is to make a note of any medical encounter, whether it's a doctor visit, a specialist consultation, a test, or phone call with a nurse practitioner. Include the date, location, name of the doctor or other provider, and the reason for the meeting. Be sure to record what happened. Did the doctor come up with a specific diagnosis? Was a preliminary course of treatment suggested, to be followed by a different one if the first didn't work? Did you get a prescription? Your log should also contain a running tally of your exposure to radiation, something few doctors record or check (avoid exceeding a lifetime limit of 6,000 rads). The third component of your chronicle is all correspondence that pertains to your care. Keep your letters as well as any written information you receive from doctors, laboratories, and pharmacies. Also make notes of any conversations with HMO administrators or medical practitioners.

DON'T forget your doctor's record.

AFTER IN-DEPTH REVIEW OF medical records of hundreds of patients, Riccardi has discovered an important fact: a doctor's record is often extremely inaccurate. Here's the story he tells about one of his clients: "I've been working with this family whose 14-year-old daughter died of cystic fibrosis in December of 1995. We've spent hours and hours reviewing all of her medical records. Sometime in April of 1994, the parents became concerned about how poorly their daughter was doing. She was in denial, not taking her medication, had lost five pounds, and there were a number of other developments. The parents took her to the doctor, described all the problems that they saw occurring, and literally begged the doctor to provide a referral to the Children's Hospital of Orange County. If you look at the doctor's clinic note for that day, there are a series of check marks next to a list of organs, indicating that they were functioning normally. And there were two words written on the page: 'Doing Well.'"

What accounts for the huge discrepancy between the parents' frightened pleas and what the doctor heard? It could have been an overdeveloped sense of medical superiority, certainty that the parents' health plan would not approve of the referral, or any number of other explanations. What's important to know is that managed care has introduced a new dynamic into a doctor's decision-making process. Rather than simply being concerned with the medical question at hand, he or she must consider a number of other factors in making a decision.

So you have to protect yourself. You not only have a right to copies of your medical record, you should claim that right. Simply ask your doctor for a copy of the clinic note when your visit is concluded. You could make this your habit, or you could make the request only when you're seeing a doctor because of a bother-

SETTING THE RECORD STRAIGHT

PART OF TAKING CHARGE OF YOUR medical records is to make sure that the master file on your health history is correct. You didn't know there was a Big Brother of the health world? There is. It's called the Medical Information Bureau, established in 1902 by medical directors at 15 life insurance companies to share medical records with other companies. The 680 member companies are willing to pool information because they want to be protected from consumers who lie about their health or omit key bits of information on their insurance applications. But, as we know, doctors' records can be inaccurate—which means what they report to insurance companies may be as well. Your treatment by a health plan and your future insurability depend upon the information at the MIB being correct.

Still, you're not likely to have a record at MIB unless you've applied for life, health, or disability insurance during the last seven years. The record on you will contain codes for 210 medical conditions and five codes for reporting nonmedical information that may affect insurers' willingness to cover you. The five lifestyle characteristics: bad driving record, participation in hazardous sports, aviation, violent or criminal activity, and possible overinsurance.

To check on the accuracy of your file, call the MIB at 617-426-3660 (or write to P.O. Box 105, Essex Station, Boston, MA 02112). If you leave your name and address, the MIB will send you forms to find out if you have a record on file and to request that it be disclosed. There's an $8 fee for each search and disclosure. You'll get a translation of coded reports, names of companies that submitted reports or made inquiries, and the names of companies that received copies of the report. If you discover incorrect information, ask the MIB how to correct it.

some health problem. In either case, read the doctor's notes. If they don't jibe with your impressions of what happened, you can do one of two things. Either ask her about it on the spot, in which case you should use the approach recommended below. Or you can write a letter to the doctor explaining that you've reviewed the clinic record as he wrote it and that it does not reflect your view of the visit. Then ask if he would incorporate your additional concerns into the record and mail you a copy of the revised medical record.

DO understand the secret message.

SUPPOSE YOU'VE BEEN bothered by increasingly severe headaches that have developed quite suddenly. Your doctor checks you out and finds nothing amiss physically. She may prescribe a drug to help you with the pain, suggest stress reduction techniques, or recommend some other palliative measure. But you're worried and want to find out what's causing the headaches. So you ask, "Don't I need an MRI scan?" The doctor says, "You're right. I'll order it." Then she writes "Patient requests MRI scan."

Guess what? That's a signal to the health plan to turn down the request. "I've been on utilization review committees, and when I saw a 'patient requests' notation I knew that meant the doctor did not find the test or referral medically necessary," explains Riccardi.

There are two explanations for why a doctor would make such a notation, knowing full well that it's likely to be turned down. The first is that the doctor simply is not being forthcoming in sharing her conclusion about your ailment. Rather than frankly discussing her reasons why she doesn't believe you need an MRI, she's using HMO shorthand to signal that she doesn't think it's necessary.

The second reason she may have framed the request this way is because she knows, all too well, that asking your health plan for an MRI is a huge headache. Maybe the plan will make her staff file reams of paper and jump through hoops to obtain the test. Maybe the doctor knows she'll be financially—or psychologically—penalized by the HMO for ordering the test. If her aversion is related to dealing with the health plan, something extremely noteworthy is happening: her medical decision is being influenced by a benefits issue. "The medical decision is, 'Do you need the MRI?' The benefit decision is, 'Is the plan going to pay for it?'" points out Riccardi. "Doctors are no longer making the best medical decisions for patients. They are couching medical decisions as benefit decisions." If you see that a doctor has put this kind of note on your record, ask why she didn't make the recommendation in her name.

DON'T become your doctor's adversary.

YOU COULD FILE A GRIEVANCE with your HMO if you and your doctor disagree about the seriousness of your problem and how to proceed. But before taking that step it's almost always worthwhile to steer a doctor away from the who's-going-to-pay-for-it benefit issue and back toward his role as a healer and patient advocate. "You want help from your doctor, not a decision from a clerk in a health plan," notes Riccardi. The way to get help is to ask for it in a very patient, organized way. Make another appointment with your doctor. Go to it equipped to take notes and ask him the following five questions:

1 Would you itemize the parts of your plan of treatment for me?

2 What specifically are the benefits associated with this course of action?

3 Okay, now what are the risks or downside to the plan?

4 What are the alternatives to this plan?

5 Will you put all of this in writing?

By reintroducing your situation in this way, you are appealing to a doctor's medical knowledge and good judgment about what should be done for your health. The discussion could result in him revising his recommendation or in you changing your mind about what's best. The most important outcome, however, is that he is reenlisted in your cause.

If he refuses again, be certain to get the denial of care or service in writing, including an explanation about why the service is not being provided. This is crucial. Many HMOs resist putting a denial in writing, which puts you in the weak position of arguing against a vaguely defined position. "You should pull out your member booklet and say, 'Give it to me in writing.' They'll say, 'We're not denying you treatment. We're deciding what's medically necessary,'" warns Jacqueline Fox, a Washington, D.C., attorney who acts as an advocate for managed care patients.

You should always document either a doctor's or an HMO's verbal denial of care or services with your own notes. Record the time, date, name of the person you're talking to, their location, and what was said as exactly as you can.

DO know who your doctor answers to.

IF YOU FIND YOU CAN'T PERSUADE your doctor to become your ally, try the same tactic on her boss. In most cases, that's not someone at an HMO, it's the medical director of an independent practice association who has a contract with your HMO. Though going up the chain of command may make you feel less hopeful about achieving your goal, remember that medical directors are doctors, too. Again, start by appealing to this part of a medical director's role, not by describing the benefits dispute. Briefly explain what your health problem is, and then explain what kind of assistance you need from the medical director. Use the word 'help' and call the director 'doctor.'

Though your tone should be respectful, don't be a wimp, either. "You should make it clear that you're not going to back down—that even though you're sick you still have the energy to pursue this," says Fox.

DON'T stay uninformed about your condition.

IF YOU'RE GETTING CONCERNED about an unaddressed health problem, you have two choices: step up your efforts to get service from your health plan or go outside the network. If you feel that your life is threatened in any way or that your situation is too unbearable to wait for the HMO, do not waste time. Go outside the network and accelerate all the steps outlined below. Don't assume the health plan knows what's best for you.

If you decide to try to get satisfaction from the plan, arm yourself as well as you can with information about your condition. You can't deal authoritatively with the people you'll be contacting unless you feel knowledgeable about what's wrong with you. The point isn't to try to act like a doctor—it's to be extremely clear about conveying your goals.

Doctors and hospitals once had a monopoly on medical information, but you now have a vast array of resources available through many channels. Here are the places you should look for information about your disease or condition:

◆**Hospitals.** Large hospitals usually sponsor a large number of support groups or can refer you to them. They can also direct you to foundations and disease centers.

◆**National societies or foundations.** If you can find one devoted to your condition, you'll find a hub for all the information you may need, from self-help materials to the latest treatment alternatives. For example, the American Foundation for Urologic Disease, based in Baltimore, Maryland, publishes a 63-page resource guide.

◆ **Internet.** Here you can find extremely sophisticated research, such as what's available on Medline (www.nlm.nih.gov), as well as down-to-earth chat boards for people with your condition. The beauty of the Web is that it covers every known and unknown condition. The downside is that it takes time to wade through and find what you need. Two excellent first stops: Healthfinder (www.healthfinder.gov), the government's listing of hundreds of health-related sites, which have been screened for accuracy, and Yahoo Health (www.yahoo.com/health/diseases_and_conditions).

◆ **Medical libraries.** These are designed for professionals, but you can navigate one with the help of a friendly librarian or doctor. Healthfinder lists the location of actual medical libraries as well as virtual

FINDING YOUR WAY ON THE WEB

WITH 8.8 MILLION REFERENCES to articles in 3,800 medical journals, Medline (www.nlm.nih.gov) is the largest scientific research database on the Web, and thus a first stop for anyone investigating his or her condition. But how do you use it efficiently? Robert Sikorski and Richard Peters, who published two articles in the *Journal of the American Medical Association* about effective search engines for Medline, suggest these five, which are accessible from their Web site (www.medsitenavigator.com):

◆ **PubMed** (www.ncbi.nlm.nih.gov/Entrez/Medline.html)

◆ **HealthGate** (www.healthgate.com/HealthGate/Medline/search.shtml)

◆ **HealthWorld Medline Search** (www.healthworld.com/Library.search.medline.htm)

◆ **Avicenna** (www.avicenna.com)

◆ **Community of Science** (www.sts.org/repos/medl/)

libraries on the Web.

As you learn more about your health problem, remember to copy or print any documents that will buttress your request for a needed consultation or service.

DO know how to handle emergencies.

ONE OF THE KEY JOBS of an HMO is to ration care. It can ration through frustration, as when it makes you jump through hoops to consult a specialist. Or it can ration by making you ask permission for certain services. The fancy name for this is precertification, and you usually have to obtain it before going to the emergency room or entering the hospital. An HMO has a twofold advantage here. Not only does it have authority to refuse you the service, it can exercise it at the last minute, when you're in a scary situation.

The best way to be prepared is to understand how an HMO decides who gets a thumbs up. Typically, an HMO nurse fields members' calls and decides who's really in immediate danger and who is not—a process known as triage. "The systems are designed to prevent unnecessary use of the emergency room. However, in doing so they oftentimes prevent *necessary* use of the emergency room. They're not giving you objective medical advice," says Dr. Sheldon Kottle, president and founder of Patients Always First, a medical information service in Tucson, Arizona. The most important thing you can do is be very articulate about the extremity of your condition. The more life-threatening it sounds, the more likely you'll get a green light.

If an HMO nurse does not want you to come to the emergency room, she's likely to propose two alternatives: a home remedy while you wait to see if the problem grows worse or an appointment with a doctor later in the day or the following day. These may well be excellent alternatives for you or your child, so consider them carefully. But if you feel you must be seen immediately, you're going to have to fight for it.

Attorney Fox recalls getting an alarmed phone call from a neighbor who had a frighteningly painful headache. The neighbor had called to get permission to go to her HMO's emergency room and been told to take some aspirin and sit in a dark room. "The chance of the headache being serious was slim, but if it was serious, she could've died," says Fox. The attorney intervened by calling the HMO's precertification nurse. At first the nurse suggested that the neighbor could go to the HMO's clinic. Fox refused, explaining that the woman needed to see a neurologist, not an internist. Finally, the nurse relented. What did the trick? "I finally said, 'Look, I'm taking her to the emergency room now. Are you going to say "No, this isn't an emergency situation, and this woman does not need a CAT scan"? Will you bear responsibility for the outcome?'" remembers Fox.

There are two lessons here. First, you must be persistent. Next, you must be authoritative and specific about what you want. If you can't pull it off—or, more likely, if you're not well enough to—ask for help. Not all of us have an attorney to turn to on such occasions, but we do have assertive relatives or friends. Ask one of them to act as your insistent advocate. Move quickly up the chain of command if you must: talk to the nurse's supervisor, the director of emergency care services and, finally, the HMO's medical director.

Once you obtain permission and are seen and treated, your job is still not done. Many of the experts I talk to say that emergency care for managed care members is much less complete than for a fee-for-service patient. As a managed care member you're likely to be released from the emergency room without any diagnostic tests having been done. If you want to know the underlying cause of the problem that drove you into the emergency room, it's up to you to pursue the matter with your primary care doctor.

DON'T overlook practical matters.

SOMETIMES THE BATTLE isn't about getting your doctor or your HMO to agree to let you see a specialist or get a test. Sometimes it's about actually getting what's been agreed to. The culprit in this case is HMO bureaucracy. Though HMOs have slashed the paperwork consumers deal with, they've wildly expanded it for doctors. "I have found the doctor's office is dealing with 30 or 40 different HMOs and PPOs at any one time. And every HMO has a different set of rules," says Janet McCarron, a community nurse in Chicago whose daughter, Ronnie, has cerebral palsy. If you've been promised a referral, follow up with the doctor's office within a week or two of being promised one. Know your HMO's protocol for obtaining the referral, in case you can help guide the doctor's staff. Ask for a copy of the referral. That way you won't find yourself barred from making or keeping an appointment with a specialist because her office hasn't received the paperwork from your HMO.

DO know your grievance procedures.

SOME EXPERTS ADVISE consumers to resist filing a grievance with their HMO for two reasons. First, it takes your medical problem out of the doctor's hands and slaps it onto a bureaucrat's desk. There, they say, you have even less chance of finding an ally. Second, grievances take too long to be addressed and solved. There's truth to both objections. But HMOs are showing an increasing interest in resolving grievances. "HMOs want to avoid liability and malpractice suits. Resolving disputes early on is one way to do it," explains Louise Trubek, senior attorney at the Center for Public Representation, a nonprofit public interest law firm in Madison, Wisconsin.

Indeed, the center recently completed a study showing that consumers may do quite well by filing a grievance, depending upon the HMO they belong to.

The highest reversal rate, meaning percentage of times the HMO reversed its decision in favor of a member, was 76 percent at MercyCare HMO. The lowest among the 23 Wisconsin HMOs examined: 19 percent at PrimeCare. HMOs' attitudes toward reversals, not surprisingly, also vary tremendously. *The Milwaukee Sentinel* reported a PrimeCare executive saying that the HMO had a low reversal rate because its customer service department did such a good job resolving complaints before they became grievances. In contrast, Compcare, which had a 71 percent reversal rate, said that the high rate reflected its efforts to listen to all the facts and to give its members fair and deliberate consideration.

Obviously, it makes sense to find out what an HMO's reversal rate is when you're choosing a plan. It's also worthwhile to know your plans' grievance procedure and the specific grievance procedures that your state imposes on HMOs. All 50 states require that HMOs maintain some kind of grievance procedure. Do you have on hand the form that must be filled out? Who is on the panel that reviews grievances? Can you appear before a grievance panel to present evidence of why care should be provided? How quickly must the HMO respond to your filing? Will their response be in writing? If you know only one thing about your HMO's grievance procedure, learn if it has a provision for an emergency appeal. In Pennsylvania, for example, if your situation is a matter of life or death, you can ask the HMO to respond within 48 hours and appeal to the state department of health for a quick answer.

DON'T get derailed by details.

THOUGH SOME HMOS ARE immediately responsive, many will not readily budge from their decision. And, plainly, there's little in the grievance process to make them. First, they won't approve you going to an out-of-network doctor to obtain a second opinion that may challenge their own doctor's first opinion. Second, a grievance committee is typically made up of HMO employees—hardly an impartial tribunal. "The deck is really stacked against most consumers in the grievance process," says Ann Torregrossa, director of Pennsylvania Health Law Project, a nonprofit public interest law firm in Philadelphia.

If you do have to file a grievance, your chances of success are more likely to be governed by how persistent you are than how right you may be. So, above all, don't be derailed by stonewalling or other obstacles. One of the first tricks to watch for: a customer service person who responds to your request to file a grievance by saying, "Oh, you have a complaint?" Do not be deflected into the complaint category in this way. "They've been absolutely trained to try to categorize your call so as to not trigger a hearing," says Torregrossa. Don't hesitate to ask to speak to a supervisor or medical director.

There are two reasons to see a grievance procedure through to its end. One is that if you ultimately decide to pursue legal action, you are often required to have exhausted all other remedies before you can bring suit. The second reason is that HMOs have key pressure points that will trigger a positive response. You may not ever find them, though, unless you go the distance.

In Pennsylvania, for example, look what happens when a consumer files an initial grievance. First, filings must be reviewed internally at the HMO, by someone who was not involved in denying care. If that grievance is denied and the member gives up, the HMO has no more headaches. But if the member files a second-level grievance, in which the member can attend the committee meeting in person and where a written record is made, the HMO has a large potential problem: second-level grievances are reported to the state. That means the information is public and could show up on various organizations' report cards. Moreover, if a second-level grievance is denied, a member can appeal to the Pennsylvania Department of Health. For those reasons, "HMOs often will fold if they're pushed to a second-level hearing," explains Torregrossa.

Be sure to follow the procedure to the letter. Make copies of the form you submit and send one to your doctor and one to the medical director of your doctor's Independent Practice Association, along with letters that explain, once again, how they can solve your problem. But don't stop there. Before the grievance committee meets, be sure to also send any letters or other information you have gathered that supports your argument for why you need the service or care you're seeking. If you can attend a hearing, consider bringing an ombudsman or attorney with you.

DO persist at the state level.

IF YOU FILE A GRIEVANCE with your HMO, you should simultaneously file one with the state department of insurance, corporations, or health, assuming their rules allow you to. State regulatory bodies vary tremendously in their responsiveness to complaints. But some are becoming far bigger activists than they used to be. In 1996, Oregon State fined two HMOs, QualMed and PacifiCare, for refusing to pay emergency room bills. Mike Hessler, head of market investigations at the Illinois Department of Insurance, believes that even HMO members who fail to get preapproval from their plan should have their treatments covered if their claims are aboveboard. Even if you don't find a friend at your state agency, you should convey your dissatisfaction for the record, so that future consumers know your plan's history. And as agencies become more forthcoming about complaint and grievance information, plans will be more concerned about such blots on their reputation.

DON'T forget you're the customer.

IF YOU'VE REACHED THE POINT where you're ready to file a grievance with your plan, you should try very hard to get your employer to demonstrate its support. HMOs battle furiously to secure corporations' health business. Though they may not seem especially responsive to you, they usually feel strongly about keeping their corporate customers happy. So a complaint or intervention by the director of your company's employee benefits department could trigger the results you want. "Patients often don't realize that employers can be staunch advocates," says Carol O'Brien, division counsel for patient advocacy at the American Medical Association in Chicago, Illinois.

Your best bet is to find the person who analyzed and selected the HMO that your company uses—often someone in employee benefits or human resources, though the chief financial officer sometimes makes this decision. Naturally, this person should feel responsibility for how the plan performs. But, just as important, this is the individual who has a relationship with one or more executives at the HMO, including the salesperson who got him to sign the contract. Briefly explain your health situation and describe your objective. Detail the steps you've taken thus far and what you plan next. Ask the director to intervene by calling her liaison at the HMO. If the answer is yes, request that the phone call be followed by a letter, with a copy sent to you.

Though this may be all that's needed to get a quick reversal of the HMO's decision, ask your employer advocate what strategies to follow if the initial intervention fails. The most likely: moving up the chain of command in both organizations. So, for example, while your director of employee benefits writes the first letter to an HMO salesperson, your company's senior vice president of administration sends the next letter to the HMO's head of sales, and your chief

ADVOCATES FOR HIRE

A FLEDGLING INDUSTRY IS springing up to help HMO members navigate their plan and obtain needed care. Note that not every one of the counselors listed below can offer advice across the country. But their guidance has already helped hundreds of sick or confused people.

◆ **CareCounsel.** Based in San Rafael, California, CareCounsel says it uses registered nurses, licensed mental health professionals, and master's level health educators with experience in managed care to advise consumers about getting their needs met in a "complicated and often unresponsive health care world." The company's services include medical information, child care, senior care, analysis of treatment plans, and acting as an advocate in disputes and care denials. Annual membership costs $92 per year (888-227-3334).

◆ **American Medical Consumers.** Run by Dr. Vincent Riccardi, this company in La Crescenta, California, helps consumers set up a personal medical record system, locate doc-

financial officer addresses the next letter to the HMO's medical director or head of legal affairs.

DO be smart about going outside the HMO.

AT A CERTAIN POINT YOU MAY feel compelled to go outside the plan for medical help rather than continuing to try to get a specialist referral or hospital precertification from your HMO. There are some important disadvantages to this decision. First and foremost, you're going to have to pay for the entire consultation or test yourself. You can—and should—try to recoup the cost from your plan later, but it's usually enormously difficult. Second, if you're turning to a specialist for a first or second opinion, for example, the plan may well ignore her advice on the grounds that she's not part of their network. "When patients con-

tors and specialists, and get the treatment they need. Annual membership costs $135 (818-957-3508).

◆ **Patients Always First.** Consumers are counseled by nurses regarding health problems, pharmaceutical questions, and doctor selection. Emergency cases, pregnancy questions, and children's issues are not covered. Based in Tucson, Arizona, the company doesn't serve consumers outside Arizona. Cost: $100 per hour or an annual subscription of $50 to $100 (602-483-9777).

◆ **Jacqueline Fox.** This Washington, D.C., attorney specializes in prelitigation resolution of health insurance disputes, ranging from denial of care to rejection of benefits claims. She charges $150 per hour (or more for emergencies) and averages four hours per client (202-966-5610).

◆ **Medicare Rights Center.** Companies can buy a Medicare Assistance Plan, a telephone counseling and educational service, for their retirees from this not-for-profit. Call 212-869-3850, ext. 19.

sult me out of network, I have to warn them, 'If you're going to see me out of your plan, there's a good chance no one will pay attention to my recommendation,'" says Dr. Riccardi.

Still, the truth is *you need the care*—and you're not getting it from your HMO. So when you've reached this point, the key is to obtain what you need in a way that's most advantageous to you. Go to the best, most experienced practitioner you can find. Experts with regional or national reputations are very hard for an HMO to ignore, no matter how chauvinistic the plan may be. For example, Larry Gelb, president of CareCounsel, a San Rafael, California, company that acts as a consumer advocate and resource, is designing a service based entirely on that premise. If you're diagnosed with cancer, CareCounsel will

RESEARCHERS FOR HIRE

IF YOU HAVE A COMPUTER and plenty of time, you can wander through acres of medical information in search of treatments for your health problem. But if you need help, there are a number of companies that will perform such information hunts for you:

◆ **AIC Services.** $50 per hour, plus computer charges. The average search costs $150 to $400 (313-996-5553).

◆ **The Health Resource.** Using your diagnosis, this company will generate a 50- to 150-page report containing mainstream and alternative treatments, as well as specialists and support groups. A report for cancer costs $350, while a noncancer condition is $250. Call 800-949-0090 or visit www.thehealthresource.com.

◆ **The Michigan Information Transfer Source (MITS).** Labor charges are $60 per hour, plus computer and phone charges. The average search costs $200 to $500 (313-763-5060).

◆ **The Institute for Health and Healing.** This San Francisco–based library of consumer information offers a range of research services. Call 415-923-3681.

◆ **Somatech.** More than a pure research service, this organization charges $50 per hour, plus computer and phone charges. A staff will interpret data and include a report offering recommendations and alternative treatments (203-364-1221).

◆ **Medical Information Line.** Geared to quickly answered questions; $1.75 per minute (900-230-4800).

help you gather together medical records and pathology slides and arrange to have them reviewed by top oncologists at Memorial Sloan-Kettering Cancer Care Center. The oncologists assess the accuracy, completeness, and quality of the diagnosis as well as the treatment recommendations of your HMO. "Then the consumer has an outside, independent review of quality from someone who has no financial interest in recommending or withholding a certain kind of treatment," says Gelb. "I would hazard a guess that when a member walks in armed with that sort of extensive research, it will get the HMO's attention." Even if your expert's recommendation doesn't sway your HMO's care decision, it should give you the leverage to ask the plan to pay for a third opinion from a specialist who is not part of the plan's network. The American Medical Association (312-464-5000) and Physicians Who Care (800-545-9305) can often provide valuable tips on second opinions and grievance strategies.

CHAPTER 7

Challenging Your
HMO

CONSUMERS ARE OFTEN stymied by an HMO's ability to say "no." But it can be necessary to second-guess a decision because you are the ultimate advocate for your own health. It's hard enough to push a regular HMO; it's even harder to deal with a Medicare HMO, because the government is footing the bill, not you or a private employer. Because the U.S. government is their customer, Medicare HMOs are a different breed of plan. The first section of this chapter describes special issues for Medicare beneficiaries who want to challenge a plan's decision. The second section is for members of regular HMOs who need to move from amicable persuasion in contesting a plan's decision to a more adversarial stance, which may include taking legal action.

GETTING THE MOST
OUT OF MEDICARE HMOS

IF YOU'RE OVER 65 you're in a highly charged
health care atmosphere. Both Medicare and
Medicare HMOs are being buffeted by so many
various and contrary changes that it would be a
mistake to consider any decision about how you
get your care permanent. And if you're a member
of a Medicare HMO, in particular, you should
stay alert to changes that government has begun

mandating, and how they affect your HMO's ability to serve you. Some of these changes will be excellent, such as information that will allow you to compare and judge plans much more easily. Others could drive HMOs to cut back on services.

Right now the most important thing to understand is the key distinction between Medicare and a Medicare HMO. When traditional Medicare disputes its responsibility for covering a special test or home health care, for example, it usually does so after you've actually gotten the test or had the home care. You still may have to wrangle over the money, but in the meantime your bodily needs have likely been met. In contrast, a Medicare HMO denies you the coverage by refusing to give you the test or the home care in the first place. Your health isn't being safeguarded while you contest the HMO's decision. So, as a Medicare HMO member, you've got to be vigilant about protecting yourself. Make sure you understand the strategies in Chapter 6 as well as the special issues pertinent to Medicare HMOs described below:

DON'T expect Uncle Sam to take care of you.

AS A MEDICARE BENEFICIARY, you have something that an ordinary HMO member doesn't: an appeals process that eventually leads to a hearing by an independent, impartial body. In theory, that's terrific. But in real life it's not necessarily an advantage. Why? The first problem is lack of information about how to challenge a decision. In March of 1997, June Gibbs Brown, inspector general of the Department of Health and Human Services, reported that many Medicare beneficiaries were never informed of their appeal rights. And, astonishingly, more than half of the HMOs examined by federal auditors did not fully comply with federal rules for handling appeals and grievances. A report by Medicare officials said that some HMOs had told Medicare patients that they could not appeal a decision regarding the termination or reduction of services. This argument was based on the idea that because an HMO had been providing a service, not denying it, members couldn't appeal the decision to curtail or stop the service.

The second problem is that Medicare HMOs can be pretty leisurely in responding to members. An HMO can take as long as 60 days to make a formal denial of care and then spend another 60 days reconsidering its denial. The worst part of this slow timetable: HMOs aren't required to continue services while their members pursue appeals. You're stuck without the home care, physical therapy, or drugs you need during a time when aggressive care could restore you to normal life. In April of 1997, HCFA announced new rules requiring that Medicare HMOs must respond to a member's appeal within 72 hours if its denial jeopardizes life, health, or the ability to regain maximum functioning. Though these new requirements are badly needed, it's hard to feel confident about Medicare HMOs complying when so few are meeting the original, more lenient standards.

Perhaps the most daunting obstacle to getting satisfaction is that the government is horribly tardy in attending to appeals cases. "Consumers commonly wait months and even years to obtain Medicare coverage for medically necessary health care," says a report issued by the Medicare Rights Center, a not-for-profit organization based in New York City. In April 1996, 224 requests for a hearing with an administrative law judge were filed nationwide, while 10,528 requests were pending, according to MRC's report on Medicare Appeals and Grievances.

DO recognize a denial of care.

A DENIAL OF CARE SEEMS obvious enough: it's when a doctor or an HMO says "No, you can't have home health care. It's not medically necessary." And of course, that is a clear-cut denial. But other refusals are far more complicated and subtle. You need to know when they're occurring so that you can take action. Here are some examples:

◆ **Termination or reduction in services.** Suppose your HMO has been providing you with 25 hours of home health care each week and then curtails the service to 15 hours. Is that a denial of services? "We say of course it is," exclaims Joe Baker, associate director of the Medicare Rights Center in New York City. "The HMO says no it isn't."

◆ **Denying that a service is covered under Medicare.** Consumer advocates report that Medicare HMOs commonly disallow services by explaining that they're not part of Medicare coverage. One member of a New Jersey Medicare HMO was prescribed biofeedback therapy by his primary care physician, who was part of the HMO's network. The HMO refused to provide the treatment, saying that biofeedback wasn't covered under the terms of its Medicare contract. In fact, Medicare does cover biofeedback therapy when more conservative treatments have failed, as was the case with this member. "Medicare HMOs are supposed to apply the same coverage guidelines. But the reality is they're not. They're applying stricter guidelines based on costs," says MRC's Baker.

◆ **Oral denials.** The tricky part of this kind of "No" is that you may not even know it happened. The straightforward case is when you ask for a test and the doctor says you don't need it. Are you getting his medical opinion—or his recognition of what your HMO will allow? The more complicated kind of denial: when a doctor doesn't describe the full range of treatment options. MRC's Baker uses the example of a member who has prostate cancer. Treatment options are numerous, but they primarily include chemotherapy, surgery, or radiation. Rather than discuss all the options, a doctor may simply recommend radiation therapy because that's what the member's HMO wants its members to try first.

◆ **Stonewalling.** This is probably the toughest kind of denial because you're never really sure if the HMO is delaying because of a bureaucratic snafu or a miscommunication—or if it's just hoping you'll just go away.

When faced with any one of these denials you need to remember two things. First, Medicare HMOs are supposed to give you a written notice of denial and an explanation of why a service was denied. But since many HMOs aren't sending these to members, you may have to ask for it. The important thing to understand: you don't need to have a written denial in hand in order to appeal an HMO's decision.

The second, very critical piece of information to know is that Medicare HMOs are required by law to provide any treatment that is covered by traditional, fee-for-service Medicare. This does not mean you can go to any doctor or provider you want if you're in a Medicare HMO—you're still restricted to the plan's providers. But it does mean that your HMO must meet the standard of care that would be available to you in traditional Medicare. And if, as described in the case above, an HMO does not have a biofeedback supplier, then it must find and pay for one.

DON'T let an out-of-town emergency wreck your budget.

THOUGH YOU CAN'T GET HEALTH CARE from any doctor or hospital you choose as a Medicare HMO member, there are two situations in which you can deviate from your HMO's list of providers. The first is when you're covered under an HMO's point-of-service benefit (called POS). It allows you to use providers other than those in the network, as long as you're willing to foot more of the bill than you would when using an in-network provider.

The second case is when you're traveling and need

either emergency or urgent care services. In a regular HMO members usually must notify the plan within a certain time frame in order to get coverage for out-of-town emergencies. But in a Medicare HMO you do not have to.

Medicare HMOs, each of which operate regular HMOs as well, often stumble over these rules. Appeals over emergency room visits were the third most frequently filed case out of 12 categories received in 1995 by the Center for Health Dispute Resolution, a group in Pittsford, New York, that reviews Medicare appeals. In a typical case described by MRC, a member of a New York Medicare HMO was visiting his daughter in Florida when he began having severe breathing difficulties. He was rushed to the hospital and a family member notified his HMO. After the member returned to New York, his HMO told him that none of the treatment would be covered because the plan had not been notified within 48 hours of the emergency. It claimed to have no record of a call. MRC explained to the member that Medicare HMOs cannot deny benefits because the HMO was not notified of emergency

ADVOCATES FOR MEDICARE BENEFICIARIES

◆ **Health Insurance Counseling** and Advocacy Program (HICAP). Free objective counseling for Medicare beneficiaries throughout the United States can be accessed by calling Eldercare Locator at 800-677-1116.

◆ **Center for Health Care Rights.** A nonprofit organization that supports HICAP, conducts research, and takes legal action to resolve health care problems affecting large numbers of people. Call 800-824-0780.

◆ **Medicare Rights Center.** A national not-for-profit group based in New York, MRC assists seniors and people with disabilities on Medicare through telephone counseling and public education. Call 212-869-3850.

treatment. After appealing the denial, the member eventually received full coverage for the treatment.

DO know how to appeal.

THE METHOD FOR CHALLENGING a Medicare HMO's decision is governed by federal law. An HMO may tell you something different from the process described below, but as MRC and many consumer advocates find, Medicare HMOs sometimes misinform their members. If you are in any doubt about how to proceed, or want to check into any federally mandated changes in the appeals process, call your regional HCFA office *(see "The Place to Go," pg. 195)*. Here are the steps to take if you want to challenge an HMO's decision:

1 Bypass the grievance level. A grievance is a complaint about the quality of services rendered. In other words, you did receive the doctor's appointment, test, or other service that you were entitled to, but you aren't happy with its quality. A lengthy delay or a brusque manner might prompt you to file a grievance with your HMO. Because grievances are not publicly reported and no one rigorously monitors how well plans respond to grievances, HMOs can settle the complaints however they want. They do not have to respond to grievances during the same time frame required for appeals, and they certainly need not forward an unresolved grievance dispute to an independent third party, as they must for an appeal. So, when you want to appeal a Medicare HMO's decision, make it crystal clear that you're filing an appeal, not a grievance. The best way to do that is to follow up an oral request to appeal with a certified letter, which you can prove was received by the HMO. You can also appeal a decision through a local Social Security office.

2 Try for an expedited decision. New HCFA rules say that when you appeal a denial-of-care decision that could jeopardize your life, health, or your ability to regain maximum function, a Medicare HMO must answer you within three days. This new time limit also applies for situations in which care has been stopped, such as when a senior is discharged from a nursing facility. Obviously, HCFA means for the rules to address many of the problems that beneficiaries have faced with Medicare HMOs. If you can make a reasonable case that a denial does impair you in the ways described above, press hard for the 72-hour decision. When you log your appeal, be sure to specify that you want a 72-hour turnaround on your appeal and explain why.

3 Get reconsideration. When you first appeal a decision, a Medicare HMO is required to "reconsider" it. You are entitled to present any evidence that supports your position either in writing or in person. Do this as completely as you possibly can by gathering information on your condition and marshaling expert opinions as described in Chapter 6. If you are asking for a very expensive procedure it may be worth your while to pay an attorney or representative to present the material for you. Even if the money amount that's involved is small you may want—or need, if you're very ill—a friend or family member to act as your advocate. If you do not qualify for a 72-hour decision, the HMO has two months in which to reconsider its decision.

4 Receive an independent review. If an HMO does not reach a decision in your favor, it's required to forward your file to the Center for Health Dispute Resolution, which has a contract from HCFA to review all of the cases in the country. The CHDR may resolve your case by picking one of four options: to uphold the plan's decision; to partially overturn it; to fully overturn it; or to forward the file to HCFA with your request for retroactive disenrollment from the plan. In 1995 the CHDR upheld HMOs' decisions in 61.5 percent of cases, while in 1996 it upheld them 65.5 percent of the time. An HMO must follow CHDR's ruling within

60 days, even if it succeeds in reopening the case. If CHDR goes against you, it must explain why and tell you how to appeal further.

5 Obtain an administrative law judge hearing. If your dispute involves a service costing a minimum of $500, you have 60 days to request an administrative law judge hearing after getting your decision from the CHDR. This is when the appeals process begins to get really bogged down. It can take a year or more to schedule a hearing. Also, administrative law judges, who are part of Social Security's administrative corps, often don't have a clear understanding of Medicare law, which causes further delays and poor decisions. Here again, you should seriously consider getting professional help in presenting your case. "In most instances you want to have an attorney there to make sure you're doing everything you can to prosecute your case," says MRC's Baker. In 1995, the average amount recovered at an ALJ hearing was nearly $3,000.

6 Take your case to the final forums. If the AJL hearing results in an unfavorable decision, you can appeal to the Department of Health and Human Services's Departmental Appeals Board. After that, your last available forum is to file an appeal in a federal district court, which you may do only if your dispute involves at least $1,000.

DO understand disenrollment procedures.

THOUGH THE GOVERNMENT-protected appeals process is supposed to be your protection against shoddy health care, your most powerful tool is actually your ability to disenroll almost immediately from any HMO that displeases you. When you leave a Medicare HMO, you don't have to join another Medicare HMO. You can return to traditional Medicare. What this means is that you will probably get the care you need much faster than by going through the appeals process. "HMOs aren't particularly generous about the home health care benefit, for example," says Baker. "You can appeal, but as a consumer advocate I'd advise you to go back to fee-for-service Medicare. Odds are, given what a doctor says about your need for it, regular Medicare will cover it."

All you need to do is notify your HMO in writing or fill out HCFA form 566 at your local Social Security office. If you write to the HMO, be sure to get proof that it received your letter. Use certified mail, with a return receipt requested. The HMO must disenroll you promptly so that you'll be covered under traditional Medicare by the first day of the month following your notification.

DON'T give up your Medigap policy too quickly.

IF YOU'RE USING TRADITIONAL Medicare, you may have a Medigap policy, which fills in for services that Medicare doesn't cover. Many folks who switch from regular Medicare to a Medicare HMO drop their Medigap or retiree insurance policies because HMOs typically provide so many extra services. That's one of the key ways that Medicare HMOs save seniors money. But there are two important reasons not to drop your Medigap policy, at least not right away. First, Medicare HMOs will be coming under greater cost pressures in the years ahead. They may stop offering many of the "extras" that you'll continue to need. Also, your Medigap or retiree policy may not be easily replaced once you drop it. So, if you later decide to switch out of a Medicare HMO into regular Medicare, you may be unable to get a Medigap policy. During the six months after your enrollment in Part B of Medicare, you can enroll in one of 10 different Medigap plans. But after that period insurance companies can refuse to issue you a policy because of your age or health status. Your ability to get a Medigap policy might be protected, however, if you live in certain states such as New York and Massachusetts, which have passed laws

THE PLACE TO GO

THE HEALTH CARE FINANCING Administration, which runs Medicare, divides the country into eight regions. Each area is managed by a regional office, which is where you can get information about rules, regulations, benefits, and Medicare HMOs in your area. HCFA regional offices are also the place you should go for help if you have been unable to resolve a dispute with a Medicare HMO or a Peer Review Organization. Here's a list of the regional offices, their phone numbers, and the areas they're responsible for:

Boston (617-565-1232). Connecticut, Maine, Massachusetts, New Hampshire, Rhode Island, Vermont

New York (212-264-3657). New York, New Jersey, Puerto Rico, Virgin Islands

Philadelphia (215-596-1332). Delaware, Washington, D.C.; Maryland, Pennsylvania, Virginia, West Virginia

Atlanta (404-331-2033). Alabama, Florida, Georgia, Kentucky, Mississippi, North Carolina, South Carolina, Tennessee

Chicago (312-353-7180). Illinois, Indiana, Michigan, Minnesota, Ohio, Wisconsin

Dallas (214-767-6401). Arkansas, Louisiana, New Mexico, Oklahoma, Texas

Kansas City (816-426-2866). Iowa, Kansas, Missouri, Nebraska

Denver (303-844-4024). Colorado, Montana, North Dakota, South Dakota, Utah, Wyoming

San Francisco (415-744-3602). Arizona, California, Guam, Hawaii, Nevada, Samoa

Seattle (206-615-2354). Alaska, Idaho, Oregon, Washington

expanding enrollment rights. Check with your state insurance department about these laws. If a Medigap policy is available, you should time your disenrollment

STATE RESOURCES ON MEDICARE

EACH STATE HAS AN INSURANCE counseling office that can advise you about conflicts with your Medicare HMO or direct you to other sources of help. Each state also has a Peer Review Organization, known as a PRO. PROs are groups of doctors and other health care professionals who essentially

STATE	STATE INSURANCE COUNSELING INFO	PEER REVIEW ORG'NS (PROS)
Alabama	800-292-8855 or 205-988-2244	Alabama Quality Assurance Fndn. 800-760-3540
Alaska	800-452-0125 or 503-222-6831	PRO-WEST 800-445-6941
Arizona	800-352-0411 or 602-861-1968	Health Services Advisory Group, Inc. 800-359-9909
Arkansas	800-482-5525 or 502-378-2320	Arkansas Foundation for Medical Care, Inc. 800-824-7586 or 800-272-5528
California	800-434-0222 or 916-323-7315	California Medical Review, Inc. 800-841-1602 or 415-882-5800
Colorado	800-544-9181 or 303-894-7499 ext. 356	Colorado Foundation for Medical Care 800-727-7086 or 303-695-3333

look over the shoulder of Medicare HMOs and other providers in order to monitor quality of care. You should make a written complaint about any Medicare-related provider to your PRO. Eventually this information may be made public or used to discipline poorly performing HMOs.

STATE	STATE INSURANCE COUNSELING INFO	PEER REVIEW ORG'NS (PROS)
Connecticut	800-994-9422	Connecticut Peer Review Organization Inc. 800-553-7590 or 203-632-2008
Delaware	800-336-9500	Health Care Excel 800-642-8686, ext. 266
District of Columbia	202-676-3900	Delmarva Foundation for Medical Care, Inc. DC: 800-645-0011 MD: 800-492-5811
Florida	800-963-5337	Florida Medical Quality Assurance, Inc. 800-844-0795 or 813-281-9024
Georgia	800-669-8387	Georgia Medical Care Foundation 800-982-0411 or 404-982-0411
Hawaii	808-586-0100	Hawaii Medical Service Association 808-948-5110

(continued)

STATE RESOURCES ON MEDICARE

STATE	STATE INSURANCE COUNSELING INFO	PEER REVIEW ORG'NS (PROS)
Idaho	S.W.: 800-247-4422 800-488-5725	PRO-WEST 800-445-6941 or 208-343-4617
Illinois	800-548-9034	Crescent Counties Foundation for Medical Care 800-647-8089 or 708-769-9600
Indiana	800-452-4800	Indiana Medical Review Organization 800-288-1499
Iowa	800-351-4664	Iowa Foundation for Medical Care 800-752-7014 or 515-223-2900
Kansas	800-432-3535	The Kansas Foundation for Medical Care 800-432-0407 or 913-273-2552
Kentucky	800-372-2973 or 502-564-7372	Kentucky Medical Review Organization 800-288-1499
Louisiana	800-259-5301 or 504-341-0828	Louisiana Health Care Review, Inc. 800-433-4958 or 504-926-6353

STATE	STATE INSURANCE COUNSELING INFO	PEER REVIEW ORG'NS (PROS)
Maine	800-750-5353	Health Care Review, Inc. 800-541-9888 or 800-528-0700
Maryland	800-243-3425 or 410-225-1074	Delmarva Foundation for Medical Care 800-492-5811 Outside MD: 800-645-0011
Massachu-setts	800-882-2003 or 617-727-7750	Massachusetts Peer Review Organization 800-252-5533 or 617-890-0011
Michigan	800-803-7174	Michigan Peer Review Organization 800-365-5899
Minnesota	800-882-6262	Foundation for Health Care Evaluation 800-444-3423
Mississippi	800-948-3090	Mississippi Foundation for Medical Care 800-844-0600 or 601-948-8894
Missouri	800-390-3330	Missouri Patient Care Review Foundation 800-347-1016

STATE RESOURCES ON MEDICARE

STATE	STATE INSURANCE COUNSELING INFO	PEER REVIEW ORG'NS (PROS)
Montana	800-332-2272	Montana-Wyoming Foundation Medical Care 800-497-8232 or 406-443-4020
Nebraska	402-471-2201	The Sunderbruch Corp.-Nebraska 800-247-3004 or 800-422-4812
Nevada	800-307-4444 or 702-367-1218	HealthInsight 800-748-6773
New Hampshire	800-852-3388 or 603-271-4642	Northeast Health Care Quality Foundation 800-772-0151 or 603-749-1641
New Jersey	800-792-8820	The PRO of New Jersey, Inc. 800-624-4557 or 908-238-5570
New Mexico	800-432-2080	New Mexico Medical Review Association 800-279-6824 or 505-842-6236
New York	800-333-4114 In NYC:	Island Peer Review Organization, Inc.

STATE	STATE INSURANCE COUNSELING INFO	PEER REVIEW ORG'NS (PROS)
	212-869-3850	800-331-7767 or 516-326-7767
North Carolina	800-443-9354	Medical Review of North Carolina 800-682-2650
North Dakota	800-247-0560	North Dakota Health Care Review, Inc. 800-472-2902 or 701-852-4231
Ohio	800-686-1578	Peer Review Systems, Inc. 800-837-0664 or 800-589-7337
Oklahoma	800-763-2828 or 405-521-6628	Oklahoma Foundation for Peer Review 800-522-3414 or 405-840-2891
Oregon	800-722-4134	Oregon Medical Professional Review Org. 503-279-0100
Pennsylvania	800-783-7067	Keystone Peer Review Organization, Inc. 800-322-1914 or 717-564-8288

(continued)

STATE RESOURCES ON MEDICARE

STATE	STATE INSURANCE COUNSELING INFO	PEER REVIEW ORG'NS (PROS)
Rhode Island	800-322-2880	Health Care Review, Inc. 800-662-5028 or 401-331-6661
South Carolina	800-868-9095 or 803-737-7500	Carolina Medical Review 800-922-3089 or 803-731-8225
South Dakota	800-822-8804 or 605-773-3656	South Dakota Foundation for Medical Care 800-658-2285
Tennessee	800-525-2816	Mid-South Foundation for Medical Care 800-489-4633
Texas	800-252-3439	Texas Medical Foundation 800-725-8315 or 512-329-6610
Utah	800-439-3805 or 801-538-3910	HealthInsight 800-274-2290
Vermont	802-828-3302	Northeast Health Care Quality Foundation 800-772-0151 or 603-749-1641

STATE	STATE INSURANCE COUNSELING INFO	PEER REVIEW ORG'NS (PROS)
Virginia	800-552-3402	Medical Society of Virginia Review Organization DC, MD, VA: 800-545-3814
Washington	800-397-4422	PRO-WEST 800-445-6941 or 206-368-8272
West Virginia	800-642-9004 or 304-558-3317	West Virginia Medical Institute, Inc. 800-642-8686, ext. 266 Charleston: 346-9864
Wisconsin	800-242-1060	Wisconsin Peer Review Organization 800-362-2320 or 608-274-1940
Wyoming	800-856-4398	Montana/Wyoming Foundation for Medical Care 800-497-8232 or 406-443-4020
American Samoa	None	Hawaii Medical Service Association/HMSA 808-948-5110

(continued)

STATE RESOURCES ON MEDICARE

STATE	STATE INSURANCE COUNSELING INFO	PEER REVIEW ORG'NS (PROS)
Guam	671-475-0262/3	Hawaii Medical Service Association/HMSA 808-948-5110
Northern	None	Hawaii Medical Service
Marian Islands		Association/HMSA 808-948-5110
Puerto Rico	809-721-8590	Puerto Rico Foundation for Medical Care 809-753-6705 or 809-753-6708
Virgin Islands	809-774-2991	Virgin Islands Medical Institute 809-778-6470

from a Medicare HMO carefully to coincide with the new coverage. That may mean staying in the HMO during the three to six months period when your Medigap policy will not cover preexisting conditions.

GETTING TOUGH WITH YOUR HEALTH PLAN

IF YOUR HMO HASN'T RESPONDED favorably to your challenge, or if you have little time to waste, you may be forced to use tougher tactics than those outlined in Chapter 6. That means being ready to pursue your claim in court. Don't make such a decision lightly. It's expensive and emotionally draining, and you're not at all assured of prevailing. One key reason: your employer, not you, struck the original deal with your HMO. "The consumer is starting right off the bat with a terrible disadvantage because he is not party to the contract with the HMO," explains Ann Torregrossa, director of the Pennsylvania Health Law Project in Philadelphia. Here's how to assess your situation and the steps you can take to prepare for legal action:

DO put a dollar figure on your problem.

THERE ARE TWO REASONS to figure out how much money your dispute is about. First, the retainer you have to pay your attorney may cost more than the service being disputed. "Out of the 200 calls we get a month, most people have a $100 to $200 issue. It's not cost effective to involve attorneys," says Mark Hiepler, a principal with Hiepler & Hiepler in Oxnard, California. A second, even more important reason to look at your dispute's price tag is that attorneys won't be interested in taking a case on a contingency basis unless the amount being contested is sizable.

DON'T omit your warning letter.

THOUGH YOU MAY HAVE ALREADY written a letter to your doctor or HMO about your problem, you must now write a slightly different one. Hiepler suggests a brief, four-paragraph letter explaining what your health problem is, how you believe it could be resolved, your belief that a treatment or procedure is medically necessary, and that you will hold the doctor and the HMO accountable for any detriment to your health. If you've already hired, or plan to hire, an attorney, say so. "A little saber-rattling goes a long way," says Carol O'Brien, the American Medical Association's division counsel for patient advocacy.

Address the letter to three people: your doctor, the HMO's chief executive officer, and the HMO's marketing director. Send each a copy by Federal Express, so that you know it will be read first. "Whether it's a big ticket item or a little ticket item, we have the person write the letter themselves from their heart, and we've had a remarkable success rate," says Hiepler.

DON'T be without an advocate.

GATHER TOGETHER AS MANY ADVOCATES on your behalf as you can. You'll need them whether you hire an attorney or not. Your employer is one of the most potent allies you can get. If you don't get a willing hand from an employee benefit manager, move on to your boss, the director of human resources, or the company attorney. Look for outside help from the consumer protection department of the state attorney general's offices or from regional patient advocacy groups. Ask your advocates to also write to the doctor, the CEO, and the marketing director on your behalf. It's not a bad idea to synchronize delivery of your letters with theirs. Their letter should again briefly outline how your problem can be resolved and what action they will take if the HMO does not help. An employer may be forced to factor in this episode when the time comes to renew its contract with the HMO. A patient advocacy group may put the details of your case in a press release or a newsletter.

DO know how to find an attorney.

UNFORTUNATELY, NOT MANY LAWYERS have the range of expertise required for bringing action against an HMO. Until recently it was especially tough to find help with a case involving a plan governed by the Employee Retirement Income Security Act of 1974, which is any health plan offered to employees as a benefit of employment. During the early 1990s HMOs were frequently successful in getting ERISA cases kicked out of state courts because they qualified for special treatment under federal law. That special treatment so undermines a patient's chances of having wrongs redressed that few attorneys were willing to take on ERISA cases. Thanks to the Department of Labor's influence, however, many of these cases are beginning to be heard in a forum where juries can award damages and give patients meaningful help. The AMA's O'Brien reports that attorneys are also finding success by arguing that ERISA plans are negligent if their cost containment measures result in a denial of necessary care.

The ideal lawyer is not only familiar with the law in this area, she's familiar with the medicine involved in your case and with HMO operations. Hiepler's firm, for example, has a doctor on staff and sends a representative to speak at many medical conventions. "Unless you have a relationship, it's very difficult to reach the famous doctors who might be able to help with a case," he explains.

Accordingly, the best way to find an attorney is to find the lawyers in previous cases that involved your medical problem or your HMO. Major medical centers which specialize in the condition you have or the procedure you're seeking will often know of attorneys in their area who are familiar with the medical problem. Call the center's department head or his staff for their suggestions. State bar associations and regional patient advocacy groups may be against your HMO. Take pains to be clear about the kind of lawyer you want if you call a bar's referral service. "There's no specialty in this area yet," says Erica Wood, associate staff director at the ABA Commission on Legal Problems of the Elderly. That means there's no prefabricated list of attorneys to choose among. You may have better luck querying a local bar association, where staffers are more familiar with local attorney's records. The AMA has developed a nationwide database, called Doctors Advisory Network, of attorneys who are health care experts and will assist doctors with their legal problems. Call Craig Samuels at 312-419-5048 at the AMA to ask for a name from this database, or call the association's division counsel for patient advocacy: Carol O'Brien (312-419-4637).

DON'T let arbitration requirements deter you.

CHANCES ARE GOOD THAT WHEN YOU signed up as a member of your HMO you signed an arbitration agreement. These compacts, which require that all future claims and disputes with a health plan be resolved through arbitration rather than in court, are on the rise. Kaiser Permanente, one of the largest health care companies in the country, has mandated the use of arbitration in all enrollment contracts since 1972. In its ideal form, arbitration has two distinct advantages over jury trials: It's cheaper and faster. But there is one very large disadvantage. Your chances of winning are poor. Arbitration is popular with medical practitioners because "it is less favorable than the courtroom for the plaintiff," noted Amy E. Elliott in a 1995 article in the *Ohio State Journal on Dispute Resolution Translation.*

The first thing to do if your health plan directs you toward arbitration is to figure out if you must resolve your differences in this manner. Typically, when a health plan has you sign an enrollment agreement, it simultaneously asks you to waive your right to a jury trial—but not always. Sometimes you have a choice. If your—or more likely, your employer's—contract requires you to arbitrate, investigate whether your state's rules will allow you to nullify it. Statutes in many states—such as Alaska, Colorado, Illinois, and Virginia—allow consumers to cancel an arbitration agreement after signing it, but usually only within a limited period of time.

There's one last way to get your day in court, even if

you signed an arbitration agreement. Find out how your state views contracts that have been negotiated by employers. Your employer has all the clout in negotiating with a health plan, while you have virtually none. Yet you're being asked to conform to a contract that you had little say-so in shaping. If your state judicial authorities believe you had no real choice in the terms of such a pact, it may see the agreement as a "contract of adhesion" and nullify it. In one case, for example, the California Supreme Court ruled that employees had to abide by an employer's agreement to arbitrate all claims. But in Oklahoma, the state's supreme court ruled that precontroversy arbitration agreements can't be enforced because they deny the courts' jurisdiction and are contrary to public policy.

If you really are stuck with arbitration, do your research. Ask the plan for information on past cases; how long they lasted and how much they cost. In most situations, you will be given some kind of choice in picking members of the arbitration panel. Ask for each arbitrator's win/loss record and how frequently he or she appears on such panels. Try to avoid picking someone who has a reason to rule against you. "If Cigna always uses Joe Arbitrator, there is an incentive for Joe Arbitrator to rule for Cigna if he wants to keep getting those assignments," explains Kathy Ventrell-Monsees, managing attorney at the American Association of Retired Persons. Because arbitration results are usually confidential, the primary arbitration resource, the American Arbitration Association in New York, New York, won't offer much assistance in researching past cases. The best person to help you choose your arbitrator and shepherd you through arbitration is an employment attorney who specializes in ERISA cases, or a personal injury lawyer who has represented patients in malpractice suits.

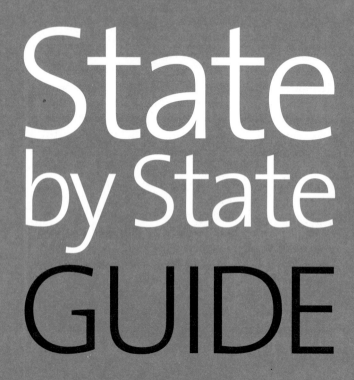

State
by State
GUIDE

HOW DOES YOUR HMO STACK UP?

YOU CAN'T GO TO ANY ONE place for a truly reliable, all-purpose rating of all HMOs. It will be years, perhaps decades, before that's possible. But you can look at the analysis already being done by different groups and organizations in order to help assess your choices. In the table beginning on page 214, I've aggregated the work of two organizations with the scores I assigned to health plans in *Newsweek*'s 1996 cover story on HMO quality. The Center for the Study of Services has long experience in grading enrollee satisfaction with plans. General Motors is one of the relatively few large corporations that are comprehensively studying plan quality and educating their employees about it. Here's how to interpret the scores from each source:

CHECKBOOK'S GUIDE TO 1997 HEALTH INSURANCE PLANS

THE CENTER FOR THE STUDY of Services, a Washington, D.C., nonprofit group that publishes Washington Consumers' *Checkbook* magazine, also rates HMOs in an annual guide. Its rating is a measure of members' satisfaction with a plan—not a grade for actual quality of medical care. This is an important indicator with some key advantages and disadvantages outlined in Chapter Two.

The Center derived its satisfaction ratings from an Office of Personnel Management survey (conducted in 1996) in which questionnaires were sent to enrollees of more than 250 plans. While the annual guide rates member satisfaction for 21 different aspects of care, including the time members get with a doctor and ability to get an appointment when sick, my table shows the rating for members' overall satisfaction with a plan. The percentage shown indicates how many members said they were extremely or very satisfied with a plan. Being "somewhat" satisfied isn't a compelling testimonial, from my point of view. And including that limp category of satisfaction just muddies the water. For example, Health Alliance HMO in Illinois has the highest rating in the state—at 94 percent—if you count the "somewhat satisfied" group in the tally. But if you chose Health Alliance, you wouldn't be selecting the Illinois plan with the greatest number of "extremely" and "very satisfied" members. That plan is United HealthCare Select, with a 74 percent rating from those two groups, compared to Health Alliance's 70 percent.

NEWSWEEK RATINGS

IF A PLAN WAS ON *NEWSWEEK*'S 1996 list of HMOs it had a chance to earn up to four dots for excellent quality of medical care. Only four out of the 43 plans listed scored that high: Fallon Community Health Plan, in Massachusetts; Harvard Community Health Plan, in Massachusetts; and two Kaiser Foundation Health Plans, in northern California and Colorado.

I surveyed HMOs on more than 20 variables in order to evaluate two key aspects of an HMO: how committed to quality a plan is and how well it's actually doing in providing superior care. Commitment to quality matters because HMOs are so new to the process of measuring their results—and reporting them in a way that is consistent with other HMOs. In this age of primitive yardsticks, concrete evidence of commitment to quality is one of the best tests of an HMO.

Actual results matter more, of course. So, in addition to asking plans for their scores on readily available measures, such as immunizations and mammograms, I asked for hard-edged, outcome data. Not many plans can yet measure or report on the mortality rates from bypass surgery, for example. But that's the direction that plans must take to gain consumer confidence. The *Newsweek* score for a plan represents the overall dot-rating that it earned after answering the survey questions. The higher the number of dots, the better.

GENERAL MOTORS

ALTHOUGH GM JUDGES HMOS on eight measurement areas, I chose five key areas for the table: preventive care, medical/surgical care, women's health, access to care, and patient satisfaction. All grades were assigned after a review of the plans' 1995 data. A score of "3" signifies superior performance, meaning that the plan's results are among the best of the plans measured. A "2" is an average score, while "1" indicates that the plan's results were among the lowest. Here is a description of what was measured in each area:

◆ **Preventive care.** How well does the HMO prevent disease? GM evaluated a plans' cancer and cholesterol screening, childhood immunization rate, prenatal care, and other wellness programs.

◆ **Medical/surgical care.** This covers the toughies: care of patients with serious chronic conditions, such as asthma, diabetes, and mental illness. The score also indicates how well a plan offers prompt and effective treatment that allows members to avoid unnecessary surgery.

◆ **Women's health.** A plan's showing in mammography and cervical cancer screening, C-sections and hysterectomies, and other women's health programs is gauged here.

◆ **Access to care.** How easy is it to actually get all the

HOW DOES YOUR HMO STACK UP?

HMOS	"CHECKBOOK"	"NEWSWEEK"
	%	
ALABAMA		
Health Partners-Birm/Hntsvl/Tsclsa	70	
Principal Hlth Care of FL-Mbl/S.AL	75	
UnitedHealthCare of AL-Anstn/Hntsvl	62	
UnitedHealthCare of Al-Birminghm	63	
UnitedHealthCare of AL-Mbl/Mtgmy/Ozrk	66	
ARIZONA		
Aetna Health Plans of Arizona	68	
CIGNA HealthCare of Arizona, Inc.-Phoenix	65	◆ ◆ ◆
FHP-most of AZ	50	
FHP-part of Mohave County	41	
FHP Health Care		◆ ◆
Humana Health Plan of Arizona	51	
Intergroup Healthcare Corp.		◆ ◆
Intergroup of Arizona, Inc.	59	
PARTNERS Hlth Plan of AZ-Tucson/S.AZ	68	
PARTNERS Hlth Plan of AZ-Yuma Co	49	
ARKANSAS		
American HMO Health Plan	60	
United HealthCare of Arkansas	65	
CALIFORNIA		
Aetna Health Plans of California, Inc.		◆ ◆

†"NEWSWEEK" RANKINGS WERE ASSIGNED TO HMOS BASED ON THEIR STATEWIDE PERFORMANCE ON QUALITY MEASURES.

care theoretically offered by an HMO? How easily can you get an appointment, get mental health care, and participate in other proactive programs? The grade in this category gives you the answer.

◆ **Patient satisfaction.** This category tells you how content members are with a plan's doctors, plan responses to inquiries, and with overall care.

GENERAL MOTORS MEDICAL PLAN GUIDE

Preventive Care	Medical/ Surgical Care	Women's Health	Access to Care	Patient Satisfaction

HOW DOES YOUR HMO STACK UP?

HMOS	"CHECKBOOK" %	"NEWSWEEK"
CALIFORNIA (continued)		
Aetna HPs of CA-Bay/Scmto/Frsno/S Crz	59	
Aetna HPs of California-S.CA	55	
Blue Shield of CA Access+HMO	50	
CaliforniaCare	58	
Care America Health Plans	60	◆
CIGNA HealthCare of CA	58	
CIGNA Medical Group Healthplan		◆ ◆
FHP Health Care-San Francisco	63	◆ ◆
Foundation Health-N.CA	48	
Health Net-Santa Monica	60	◆ ◆ ◆
Kaiser Foundation HealthPlan, Inc. (Northern)	71	◆ ◆ ◆ ◆
Kaiser Foundation HealthPlan, Inc. (Southern)	69	◆ ◆ ◆
KP Northeast-Oakland		
Maxicare Northern California	57	
Maxicare Southern California	55	
National HMO Health Plan	58	
Omni Healthcare	60	
PacifiCare of California	64	◆ ◆
PruCare of California		◆ ◆
COLORADO		
FHP of Colorado-High	58	◆ ◆ ◆ †
FHP of Colorado-Std	61	◆ ◆ ◆ †
HMO Colorado-Denver		
HMO Colorado/Nevada	57	
Kaiser Foundation Health Plan of Colorado	79	◆ ◆ ◆
QualMed Plans for Health	59	
Rocky Mountain HMO	71	
CONNECTICUT		
BlueCare-North Haven		
ConnectiCare	85	

GENERAL MOTORS MEDICAL PLAN GUIDE

Preventive Care	Medical/ Surgical Care	Women's Health	Access to Care	Patient Satisfaction
1	2	2	3	3
2	2	2	1	3
3	3	3	3	3
2	3	2	3	3
3	3	3	3	3
1	N/A	1	1	1
2	2	3	1	N/A
3	2	3	3	3
2	2	2	1	2

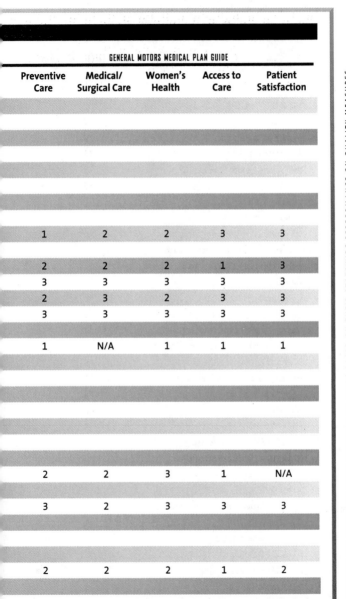

†"NEWSWEEK" RANKINGS WERE ASSIGNED TO HMOS BASED ON THEIR STATEWIDE PERFORMANCE ON QUALITY MEASURES.

HOW DOES YOUR HMO STACK UP?

HMOS	"CHECKBOOK" %	"NEWSWEEK"
CONNECTICUT (continued)		
Harvard CHP	67	
Health New England	74	
Kaiser Permanente	74	
Physicians Health Services/CT	79	
US Healthcare	65	
DELAWARE		
AmeriHealth HMO, Inc.	69	
US Healthcare-Wilmington	58	
DISTRICT OF COLUMBIA		
Aetna HPs of the Mid-Atlantic	61	
CareFirst	59	
Chesapeake Health Plan	56	
CIGNA HealthCare Mid-Atlantic	55	
George Washington Univ HP-High	72	
George Washington Univ HP-Std	58	
Humana Group Health Plan-High	48	
Humana Group Health Plan-Std	44	
Kaiser Permanente	77	
M.D.IPA	62	
NYLCARE/Mid-Atlantic-High	74	
NYLCARE/Mid-Atlantic-Std	62	
Prudential Health HMO MidAtl	60	
US Healthcare	61	
FLORIDA		
AV-MED-Broward/Dade/Palm Beach	70	◆ ◆ †
AV-Med-Gainesville	74	◆ ◆ †
AV-MED-Jacksonville	70	◆ ◆ †
AV-MED-Orlando	65	◆ ◆ †
AV-MED-Tampa Bay area	62	◆ ◆ †
Capital Health Plan	78	

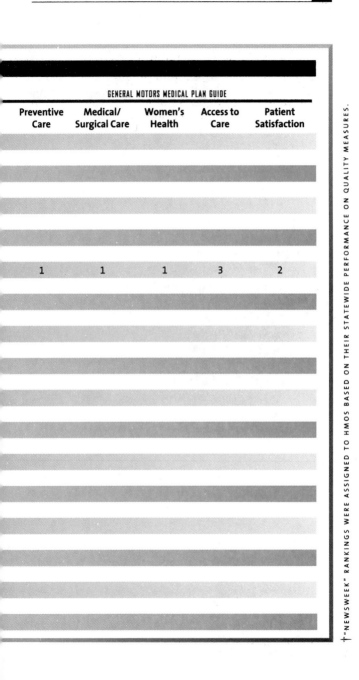

GENERAL MOTORS MEDICAL PLAN GUIDE

Preventive Care	Medical/ Surgical Care	Women's Health	Access to Care	Patient Satisfaction
1	1	1	3	2

†"NEWSWEEK" RANKINGS WERE ASSIGNED TO HMOS BASED ON THEIR STATEWIDE PERFORMANCE ON QUALITY MEASURES.

HOW DOES YOUR HMO STACK UP?

HMOS	"CHECKBOOK"	"NEWSWEEK"
	%	
FLORIDA (continued)		
CIGNA HealthCare of Florida		◆ ◆
HEALTH OPTIONS, INC.-Jacksonville		
Health Options-Broward/Dade Cos	51	
Health Options-Jksnville/Gnsville	68	
Health Options-Palm Bch/Martin Cos	53	
Health Options-Tampa Bay	59	
HIP Health Plan of Florida-Hollywood	60	
Humana Medical Plan-Daytona	49	
Humana-Brwrd/Dade/Palm Beach Cos	46	
Humana-Jksnville/Orlando areas	51	
Humana-Tampa Bay area	56	
PCA Health Plans of Florida	39	
Principal Hlth Care of FL-Pensacola	75	
Prudential HlthCare HMO-Brwd/Dade/Palm Bch	69	
Prudential HlthCare HMO-C. FL area	71	
Prudential HlthCare HMO-Jcksnville area	71	
GEORGIA		
Aetna HPs of Georgia, Inc.	57	
Blue Choice-Atlanta		
Kaiser Permanente Georgia	66	◆ ◆ ◆
Prudential HealthCare HMO of Atlanta	63	
United HealthCare of Georgia	68	
GUAM		
FHP	47	
Guam Memorial Health Plan-High	53	
Health Maintenance Life	59	
HAWAII		
HMSA	61	
HMSA's CHP	57	
Kaiser HI	55	◆ ◆ ◆

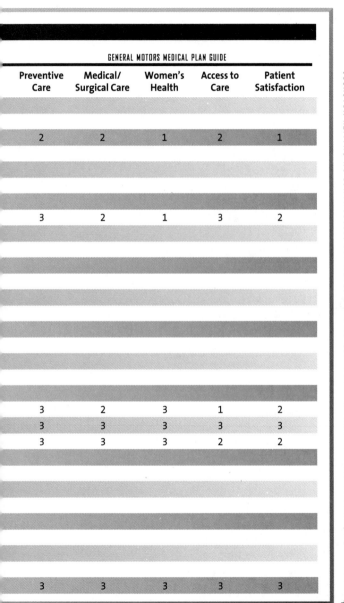

	GENERAL MOTORS MEDICAL PLAN GUIDE			
Preventive Care	Medical/ Surgical Care	Women's Health	Access to Care	Patient Satisfaction
2	2	1	2	1
3	2	1	3	2
3	2	3	1	2
3	3	3	3	3
3	3	3	2	2
3	3	3	3	3

HOW DOES YOUR HMO STACK UP?

HMOS	"CHECKBOOK"	"NEWSWEEK"
	%	
IDAHO		
Group Health Northwest	71	
HMO Blue-Southwestern ID	57	
QualMed WA Hlth Plan-N. ID/Boise	64	
ILLINOIS		
Aetna HPs of the Midwest	54	
BCI HMO, Inc.	59	
BlueCHOICE	61	
Chicago HMO Ltd	56	
FHP of Illinois, Inc.	63	
Group Health Plan	63	
Health Alliance	70	
HMO Illinois-Oak Brook		
Humana Health Plan Inc.	49	
Humana HealthChicago	52	
Maxicare IL-Chic/Moln/Peor/Rckfd	45	
Maxicare IL-Springfield area	64	
PARTNERS HMO	75	
Personal Care's HMO	71	
Principal St. Louis	71	
The Anchor Plan-Rush Prudential-Chicago		
Rush Prudential HMO, Inc.	58	◆ ◆
Share Health Plan of Illinois	59	
United HealthCare Select	74	
INDIANA		
Aetna HPs of the Midwest	54	
BCI HMO, Inc.	59	
FHP of Illinois, Inc.-Lake County	63	
Health Alliance HMO	70	
Humana Care Plan-S. Indiana	60	
Humana Health Plan-Lake County	49	

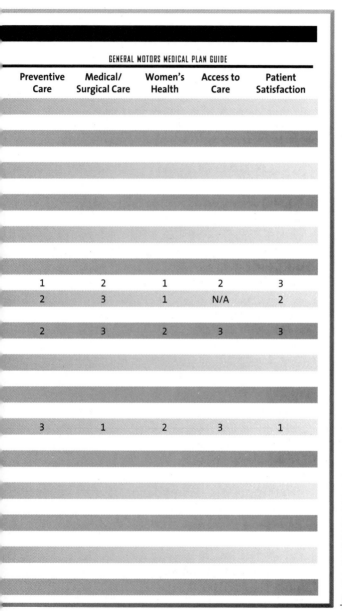

GENERAL MOTORS MEDICAL PLAN GUIDE				
Preventive Care	Medical/ Surgical Care	Women's Health	Access to Care	Patient Satisfaction
1	2	1	2	3
2	3	1	N/A	2
2	3	2	3	3
3	1	2	3	1

HOW DOES YOUR HMO STACK UP?

HMOS	"CHECKBOOK"	"NEWSWEEK"
	%	
INDIANA (continued)		
Humana Health Plan-S. Indiana	51	
Humana HealthChicago	52	
Maxicare IL-Lake County	45	
Maxicare Indiana/Indianapolis	58	
Rush Prudential HMO, Inc.	58	
The M Plan-Indianapolis	73	
Welborn HMO	79	
IOWA		
Care Choices	73	
Maxicare IL-Clntn/Msctn/Scott Cos	45	
Principal Hlth Care of NE-C. Blfs	63	
Principal Iowa	61	
UnitedHealthCare of Midlands	68	
KANSAS		
Humana Kansas City, Inc.	54	
Kaiser Permanente	74	
Principal Hlth Care of KC-KC/Topeka	73	
KENTUCKY		
Advantage Care, Inc.	81	
Aetna HPs of OH-Brne/Cmpbl/Gmt/Kntn Cos	63	
FHP of Ohio, Inc.-N.Kentucky	61	
HealthWise of Kentucky	77	
Humana Care Plan-Lexington area	55	
Humana Care Plan-Louisville area	60	
Humana Health Plan-Lexington/Louisville	51	
Prudential HlthCare HMO Cin-N.KY	66	
LOUISIANA		
Aetna HPs of LA-New Orleans area	52	
Comm Hlth Ntwrk of LA-Baton Rouge/Lafayette	77	
Comm Hlth Ntwrk of LA-New Orleans area	66	

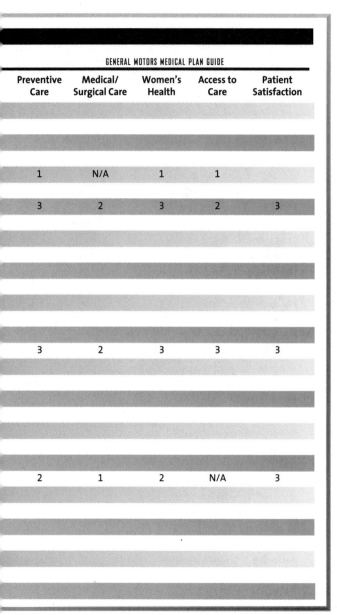

GENERAL MOTORS MEDICAL PLAN GUIDE

Preventive Care	Medical/ Surgical Care	Women's Health	Access to Care	Patient Satisfaction
1	N/A	1	1	
3	2	3	2	3
3	2	3	3	3
2	1	2	N/A	3

† "NEWSWEEK" RANKINGS WERE ASSIGNED TO HMOS BASED ON THEIR STATEWIDE PERFORMANCE ON QUALITY MEASURES.

HOW DOES YOUR HMO STACK UP?

HMOS	"CHECKBOOK"	"NEWSWEEK"
	%	
LOUISIANA (continued)		
Maxicare Louisiana	55	
Principal LA	56	
MARYLAND		
Aetna HPs Mid-Atl-Balt/Wsh/StMry/Wicmo/Wich	58	
Aetna HPs Mid-Atlantic-DC area	61	
CareFirst	59	
Chesapeake Health Plan	56	
CIGNA HealthCare Mid-Atlantic	55	
Columbia Medical Plan	69	
Free State Health Plan-Owings Mills	66	
George Washington Univ HP-High	72	
George Washington Univ HP-Std	58	
Humana Group Health Plan-High	48	
Humana Group Health Plan-Std	44	
Kaiser Foundation HP of the Mid-Atl States	77	◆◆◆
M.D.Individual Practice Assn., Inc.-Rockville	62	
NYLCare-Greenbelt		◆◆◆†
NYLCARE/Mid-Atlantic-High	74	◆◆◆†
NYLCARE/Mid-Atlantic-Std	62	◆◆◆†
Prudential Health HMO MidAtl	60	
US Healthcare	61	
MASSACHUSETTS		
BCBSMA - HMO Blue/Boston		◆◆◆
Community Health Plan	72	
Coordinated Health Partners	75	
Fallon Community Health Plan Worcester	74	◆◆◆◆
Harvard Community Health Plan-Brookline	67	◆◆◆◆
Harvard Pilgrim Health Care-NE	74	
Health New England	74	
Healthsource CMHC	80	

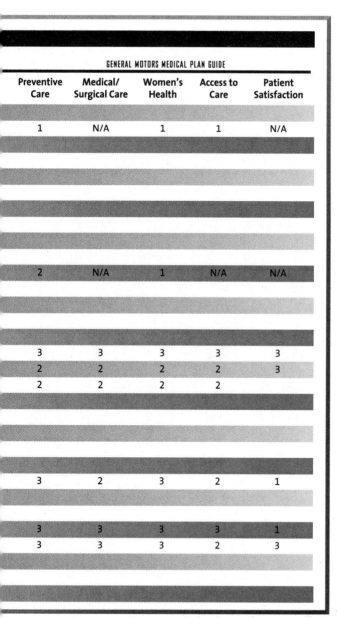

	GENERAL MOTORS MEDICAL PLAN GUIDE			
Preventive Care	**Medical/ Surgical Care**	**Women's Health**	**Access to Care**	**Patient Satisfaction**
1	N/A	1	1	N/A
2	N/A	1	N/A	N/A
3	3	3	3	3
2	2	2	2	3
2	2	2	2	
3	2	3	2	1
3	3	3	3	1
3	3	3	2	3

HOW DOES YOUR HMO STACK UP?

HMOS	"CHECKBOOK"	"NEWSWEEK"
	%	
MASSACHUSETTS (continued)		
Kaiser Permanente	71	
Matthew Thornton Health Plan	70	
Pilgrim HealthCare, Inc.		◆ ◆ ◆
Tufts Health Plan		◆ ◆ ◆
United HPs of New England	76	
US Healthcare MA		
MICHIGAN		
Blue Care Network East MI-Flint	71	
Blue Care Network East MI-Saginaw	64	
Blue Care Network Health Central-Lansing	59	
Blue Care Network-SE Michigan-Southfield	60	
Blue Care Network-Great Lakes/Grand Rapids		
Blue Care Network-Great Lakes-N.MI	67	
Blue Care Network-Great Lakes-SW MI	66	
Blue Care Network-Great Lakes-W.MI	76	
CARE Choices-Farmington Hills		
Care Choices-East/Central Michigan	68	
Care Choices-Western Michigan	81	
Health Alliance Plan-Detroit	62	
HealthPLUSof MI-Flint		
M-CARE	75	
Medical Value Plan	84	
OmniCare Health Plan/Detroit	51	
Physicians HP-Kalamazoo/SW MI	65	
Physicians HP (Michigan, Inc.)-Lansing	74	
Priority Health-Grand Rapids	80	
SelectCare HMO-Troy	62	
MINNESOTA		
Blue PLUS (BCBS of MN)-St. Paul		
HealthPartners Health Plan-Minneapolis	65	

GENERAL MOTORS MEDICAL PLAN GUIDE				
Preventive Care	Medical/ Surgical Care	Women's Health	Access to Care	Patient Satisfaction
2	1	1	3	
3	3	3	1	2
1	3	1	2	1
1	1	1	1	2
3	2	3	2	3
3	3	3	3	1
3	1	2	2	1
N/A	N/A	1	N/A	3
1	2	2	2	3
1	1	2	3	3
1	1	1	1	2
3	2	3	3	2
3	3	3	1	3

† "NEWSWEEK" RANKINGS WERE ASSIGNED TO HMOS BASED ON THEIR STATEWIDE PERFORMANCE ON QUALITY MEASURES.

HOW DOES YOUR HMO STACK UP?

HMOS	"CHECKBOOK"	"NEWSWEEK"
	%	
MINNESOTA (continued)		
HealthPartners Select-High	73	
HealthPartners Selct-Std	75	
Medica Primary	58	
MISSOURI		
BlueCHOICE	61	
Group Health Plan-St.Louis	63	
Humana Kansas City-High-KC area	54	
Kaiser Permanente Kansas City	74	
PARTNERS HMO-St. Louis area	75	
Principal Health Care of KC	73	
Principal St. Louis	71	
Total Health Care (BCBS-Kansas)-Kansas City		
United HealthCare Choice	74	
United HealthCare Select	74	
NEBRASKA		
Care Choices	73	
Principal Health Care of NE	63	
United HealthCare of Midlands	68	
NEVADA		
FHP	41	
Health Plan of Nevada	48	
NEW HAMPSHIRE		
Harvard CHP	67	
Healthsource New Hampshire	68	
Kaiser Permanente	71	
Matthew Thornton Health Plan	70	
US Healthcare	59	
NEW JERSEY		
AmeriHealth HMO, Inc.	55	
GHI Health Plan	55	

GENERAL MOTORS MEDICAL PLAN GUIDE

Preventive Care	Medical/ Surgical Care	Women's Health	Access to Care	Patient Satisfaction
2	2	2	2	2
3	2	3	3	3
1	3	1	2	1
	1	1		2

†"NEWSWEEK" RANKINGS WERE ASSIGNED TO HMOS BASED ON THEIR STATEWIDE PERFORMANCE ON QUALITY MEASURES.

HOW DOES YOUR HMO STACK UP?

HMOS	"CHECKBOOK"	"NEWSWEEK"
	%	
NEW JERSEY (continued)		
HIP Health Plan of New Jersey-N. Brunswick	65	
US Healthcare NJ-High	62	
US Healthcare NJ-Std	59	◆ ◆ ◆
NEW MEXICO		
FHP NM	49	
Cigna Lovelace Health Plan	70	
Presbyterian Health Plan	63	
QualMed Plans for Health	71	
NEW YORK		
Blue Choice-Rochester area	75	
BlueChoice HMO-Downstate area	48	
C.D.P.H.P.	84	
CHP/Hudson Valley Region	71	
Community Blue-Western NY	67	
Community Health Plan-Latham	76	◆ ◆ ◆
GHI Health Plan	55	
Harvard CHP	67	
HEALTH CARE PLAN-Buffalo	70	
HIP of Greater New York-NYC	52	◆ ◆
HMO-CNY-Aubrn/Crtlnd/Fltn/Syrcse	74	
HMO-CNY-Ithaca/Elmira	58	
Independent Hlth-Metro Hudson	67	◆ ◆ ◆ †
Independent Hlth-Western NY	69	◆ ◆ ◆ †
Kaiser Permanente New York-White Plains	64	
MVP Health Plan-Central-Northrn Rgn	67	◆ ◆ ◆ †
MVP Health Plan-Eastern Region	74	◆ ◆ ◆ †
MVP Health Plan-Mid-Hudson Region	68	◆ ◆ ◆ †
NYLCare Health Plans	50	
Oxford Health Plans	68	◆ ◆ ◆
PHP/Slocum-Dickson	62	

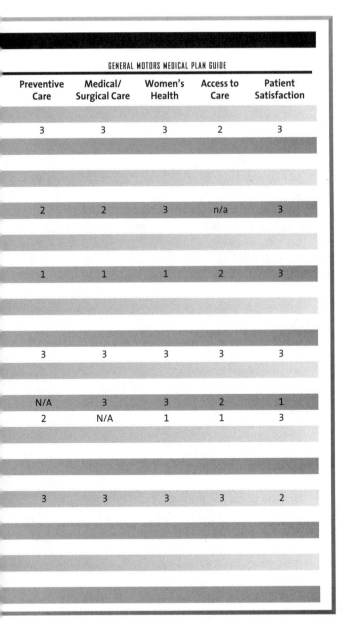

GENERAL MOTORS MEDICAL PLAN GUIDE				
Preventive Care	Medical/ Surgical Care	Women's Health	Access to Care	Patient Satisfaction
3	3	3	2	3
2	2	3	n/a	3
1	1	1	2	3
3	3	3	3	3
N/A	3	3	2	1
2	N/A	1	1	3
3	3	3	3	2

† "NEWSWEEK" RANKINGS WERE ASSIGNED TO HMOS BASED ON THEIR STATEWIDE PERFORMANCE ON QUALITY MEASURES.

HOW DOES YOUR HMO STACK UP?

HMOS	"CHECKBOOK"	"NEWSWEEK"
	%	
NEW YORK (continued)		
Preferred Care	72	
Prepaid Health Plan-Syracuse-Utica-Binghamton/Baldwinsville	68	
US Healthcare NY	60	◆ ◆
Vytra Healthcare	63	
WellCare of NY-Hudson Valley Region	59	
NORTH CAROLINA		
Kaiser Permanente NC-Oakland	65	
Maxicare North Carolina	55	
PARTNERS NHP of North Carolina	74	
PHP, Inc.	71	
Prudential HealthCare HMO-NC	61	
NORTH DAKOTA		
HealthPartners Health Plan	65	
HealthPartners Select-High	73	
HealthPartners Select-Std	75	
OHIO		
Aetna HPs of Ohio, Inc.	63	
Choice Care		◆ ◆
CHP of Ohio	73	
CIGNA HealthCare	69	
DayMed Health Maintenance Plan	44	
FHP of Ohio, Inc.	61	
Health Maintenance Plan (HMP)	70	
Health Plan Upper Ohio Valley	72	
HMO Health Ohio (BCBS of Ohio)-Akron		
HMO Health Ohio-Central Ohio	61	
HMO Health Ohio-Northeast Ohio	63	
HMO Health Ohio-NW/SW Ohio	64	
Kaiser Permanente Ohio-Oakland	66	

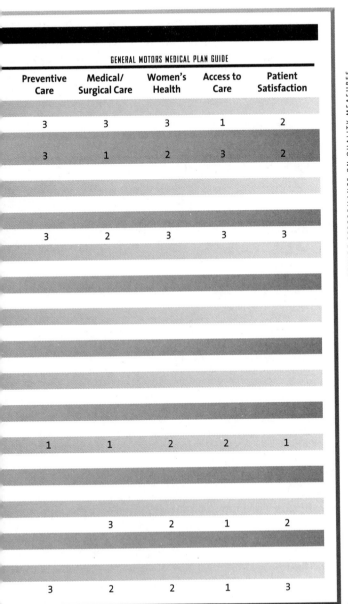

	GENERAL MOTORS MEDICAL PLAN GUIDE			
Preventive Care	Medical/ Surgical Care	Women's Health	Access to Care	Patient Satisfaction
3	3	3	1	2
3	1	2	3	2
3	2	3	3	3
1	1	2	2	1
	3	2	1	2
3	2	2	1	3

† "NEWSWEEK" RANKINGS WERE ASSIGNED TO HMOS BASED ON THEIR STATEWIDE PERFORMANCE ON QUALITY MEASURES.

HOW DOES YOUR HMO STACK UP?

HMOS	"CHECKBOOK" %	"NEWSWEEK"
OHIO (continued)		
Kaiser Foundation Health Plan of Ohio		◆ ◆ ◆
Medical Value Plan	84	
Prudential HlthCare-HMO Cincinatti-SW area	66	
Prudential HlthCare HMO-Columbus	70	
Prudential Northern OH-Cleveland/Akron	55	
United Health Care of Ohio-Central/NE/S.Central	70	
United Health Care of Ohio-Dayton	68	
OKLAHOMA		
Blue Lincs HMO-Oklahoma City	53	
PacifiCare of OK-Tulsa area	64	
PacifiCare OK-OK City/SW OK	56	
Prucare of Oklahoma City PLUS		
Prudential of Oklahoma City	64	
Prudential Tulsa	69	
OREGON		
HMO Oregon (BCBS)		◆ ◆
Kaiser Foundation HP of the Northwest	63	◆ ◆ ◆
PacifiCare of Oregon	49	
QualMed Oregon Health Plan	59	
SelectCare	53	
PENNSYLVANIA		
Advantage Health Plan-PA	46	
Aetna HP/Cntrl & E.PA-Harrisburg	72	
Aetna HP/Cntrl & E.PA-Phil/Rdng	65	
First Priority Health	65	
Free State Health Plan	66	
Geisinger Health Plan	71	
HealthAmerica PA-Grt Pittsburgh area	66	◆ ◆ ◆
HealthAmerica PA-Central PA		◆ ◆ ◆
HealthAmerica PA-South Central PA	74	

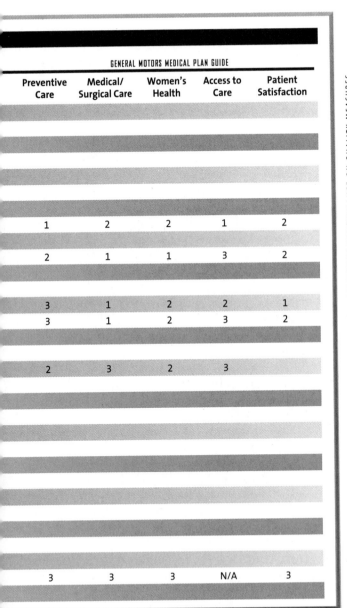

GENERAL MOTORS MEDICAL PLAN GUIDE

Preventive Care	Medical/ Surgical Care	Women's Health	Access to Care	Patient Satisfaction
1	2	2	1	2
2	1	1	3	2
3	1	2	2	1
3	1	2	3	2
2	3	2	3	
3	3	3	N/A	3

† "NEWSWEEK" RANKINGS WERE ASSIGNED TO HMOS BASED ON THEIR STATEWIDE PERFORMANCE ON QUALITY MEASURES.

HOW DOES YOUR HMO STACK UP?

HMOS	"CHECKBOOK"	"NEWSWEEK"
	%	
PENNSYLVANIA (continued)		
HealthGuard	69	
HMO-CNY	58	
Keystone Blue-Pittsburgh area	67	
Keystone Health Plan East	62	
Keystone HP Central-Harrisburg area	62	
Keystone HP Central-Lehigh Valley area	55	
US Healthcare-Blue Bell		◆ ◆ ◆
US Healthcare PA-High-Philadelphia area	62	
US Healthcare PA-Std-Philadelphia area	53	
US Healthcare-High-Ptsbrg/Hrsbrg/NE PA	68	
PUERTO RICO		
PCA-Puerto Rico/Miami		
Triple-S	74	
RHODE ISLAND		
Coordinated Health Partners	65	
Harvard CHP	67	
Harvard Pilgrim Health Care-NE	74	
United HPs of New England	76	
SOUTH CAROLINA		
Companion HealthCare	53	
Healthsource SC-Charlestown/Upstate	75	
Maxicare NC-Chester/York Cos	55	
Maxicare South Carolina	56	
PARTNERS NHP of NC-Upstate SC	74	
Prudential HlthCare HMO-NC-Yrk Co	61	
SOUTH DAKOTA		
Care Choices	73	
TENNESSEE		
CIGNA HealthCare of Memphis		
Healthsource Tennessee, Inc.	69	

Preventive Care	Medical/ Surgical Care	Women's Health	Access to Care	Patient Satisfaction
2	2	2	3	3
				1
2	2	3	3	1

GENERAL MOTORS MEDICAL PLAN GUIDE

†"NEWSWEEK" RANKINGS WERE ASSIGNED TO HMOS BASED ON THEIR STATEWIDE PERFORMANCE ON QUALITY MEASURES.

HOW DOES YOUR HMO STACK UP?

HMOS	"CHECKBOOK" %	"NEWSWEEK"
TENNESSEE (continued)		
Prucare of Memphis PLUS		
Prucare of Nashville PLUS		
Prudential HlthCare HMO-Memphis	59	
Prudential HlthCare HMO-Nashvillel area	61	
United HealthCare of Tennessee	67	
TEXAS		
Aetna Health Plans of North Texas	64	
CIGNA HealthCare of North Texas-Bloomfield		
FHP NM-El Paso area	49	
FIRSTCARE	60	
Harris Methodist Health Plan	61	◆ ◆
Humana Health Plan of TX-Austin	29	
Humana Health Plan of TX-San Antonio	53	
Humana of Corpus Christi	58	
Kaiser Permanente Texas-Oakland	61	
MetraHealth Care Plan TX	3	
NYLCare Health Plans SW	54	◆ †
NYLCARE HP of the Gulf Coast	60	◆ †
PacifiCare of TX-San Antonio area	61	
PCA Health Plans of Texas	59	
Principal Health Care of Texas	61	
Prudential HlthCare HMO-Austin	51	
Prudential HlthCare HMO-Houston	54	
Prudential HlthCare HMO-San Antonio	71	
Scott and White Health Plan	84	
UTAH		
FHP Utah	51	
VERMONT		
Harvard CHP	67	
Kaiser Permanente	71	

Preventive Care	Medical/ Surgical Care	Women's Health	Access to Care	Patient Satisfaction
1	2	1	2	1
1	1	1	1	1
1	3	1	3	2
1	3	2	1	2
1	3	2	N/A	1
N/A	1	1	3	1
1	1	1	1	2
3	1	3	3	3
2	3	3	1	2

GENERAL MOTORS MEDICAL PLAN GUIDE

† "NEWSWEEK" RANKINGS WERE ASSIGNED TO HMOS BASED ON THEIR STATEWIDE PERFORMANCE ON QUALITY MEASURES.

HOW DOES YOUR HMO STACK UP?

HMOS	"CHECKBOOK" %	"NEWSWEEK"
VIRGINIA		
Aetna HPs Mid-Atl-N.Virginia area	61	
Chesapeake Health Plan	56	
CIGNA HlthCare Mid-Atl-N.VA	55	
CIGNA HlthCare-Pnsla/SS Hmpt Rd	67	
CIGNA HlthCare-Rich/Tri-City area	66	
George Washington Univ HP-High	72	
George Washington Univ HP-Std	58	
HMO VA-Peninsula/Hampton Rds	55	
HMO VA-Rich/Tri-City/Chville/Frdbrg	51	
Humana Group Health Plan-High	48	
Humana Group Health Plan-Std	44	
Kaiser Permanente	77	
M.D.IPA	62	
NYLCARE/Mid-Atlantic-High	74	
NYLCARE/Mid-Atlantic-Std	62	
OPTIMA Health Plan	67	
PARTNERS NHP of NC-SW VA	74	
Prudential Health HMO MidAtl	60	
Prudential Richmond	63	
WASHINGTON		
Group Health Coop. of Puget Sound-Seattle	65	◆ ◆ ◆
Group Health Northwest-Spokane	71	
Kaiser Permanente	63	
Kitsap Physicians Service-High	75	
Kitsap Physicians Service-Std	74	
PacifiCare of Oregon-Clark Co	49	
PacifiCare of Washington	55	
QualMed Oregon HP-Clrk/Cwltz Cos	59	
QualMed Washington Health Plan	64	
SelectCare	53	

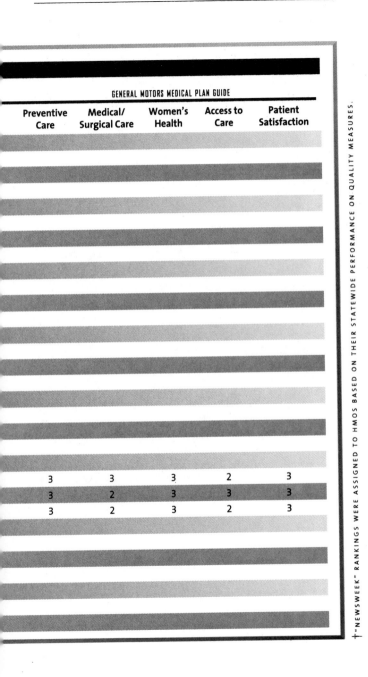

GENERAL MOTORS MEDICAL PLAN GUIDE

Preventive Care	Medical/ Surgical Care	Women's Health	Access to Care	Patient Satisfaction
3	3	3	2	3
3	2	3	3	3
3	2	3	2	3

†"NEWSWEEK" RANKINGS WERE ASSIGNED TO HMOS BASED ON THEIR STATEWIDE PERFORMANCE ON QUALITY MEASURES.

HOW DOES YOUR HMO STACK UP?

HMOS	"CHECKBOOK" %	"NEWSWEEK"
WEST VIRGINIA		
Free State Health Plan	66	
Health Plan Upper Ohio Valley	72	
WISCONSIN		
Atrium (formerly HMO Midwest)	79	
Chicago HMO Ltd	56	
Compcare Health Services	53	
DeanCareHMO-Middletown	80	
Family Health Plan-Milwaukee	69	
Group Health Coop. (Sun Prairie)-Madison	80	
HealthPartners Health Plan	65	
HealthPartners Select-High	73	
HealthPartners Select-Std	75	
Humana WI Health Organization	62	
Maxicare Wisconsin	55	
Medica Primary	58	
Physicians Plus HMO	79	
PrimeCare Health Plan, Inc.	59	
PrimeCare/United Health Care		
Unity Health Plans	65	

†"NEWSWEEK" RANKINGS WERE ASSIGNED TO HMOS BASED ON THEIR STATEWIDE PERFORMANCE ON QUALITY MEASURES.